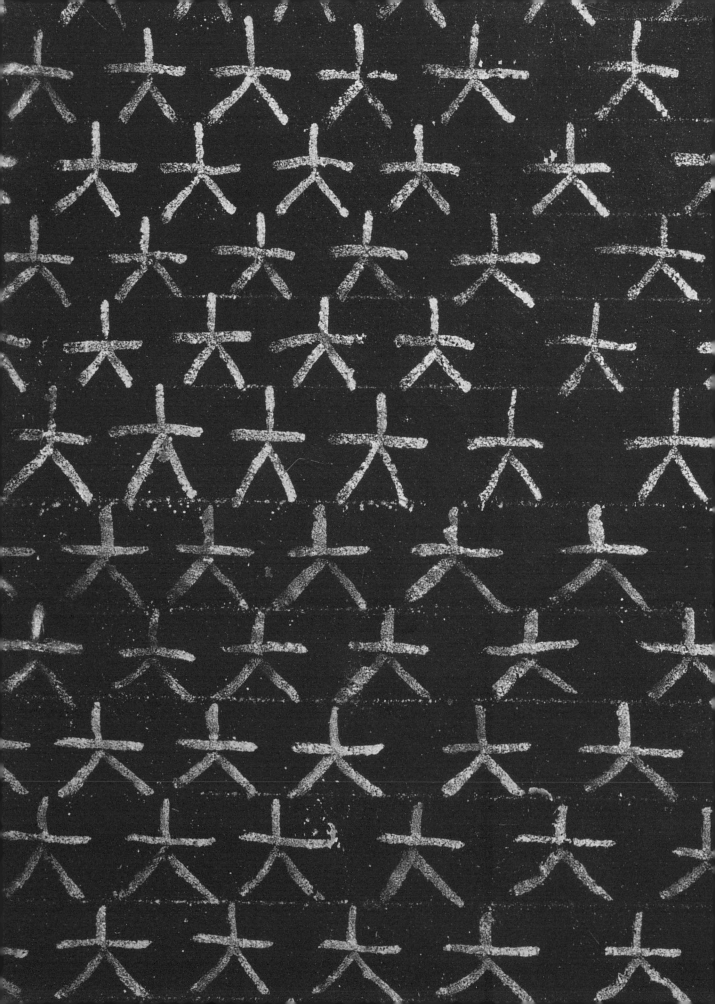

# IN THE TOMB OF NEFERTARI

# In the Tomb of
# Nefertari
# Conservation of the
# Wall Paintings

The J. Paul Getty Museum and The Getty Conservation Institute   1992

Kurt Hauser, Designer
Elizabeth Burke Kahn, Production Coordinator
Eileen Delson, Production Artist
Beverly Lazor-Bahr, Illustrator

Typography by Wilsted & Taylor, Oakland, California
Printing by Westland Graphics, Burbank, California

Library of Congress Cataloging-in-Publication Data

In the tomb of Nefertari : conservation of the wall paintings.
    p.    cm.
    "Published on the occasion of an exhibition at the J. Paul Getty
Museum, Malibu, November 12, 1992–February 21, 1993. The exhibition
was organized by the museum in cooperation with the Getty
Conservation Institute"—T.p. verso.
    Includes bibliographical references.
    ISBN 0-89236-229-4 (paper)
    1. Mural painting and decoration. Egyptian—Conservation and
restoration—Egypt—Thebes (Egypt : Extinct city)—Exhibitions.
2. Mural painting and decoration, Ancient—Conservation and
restoration—Egypt—Thebes (Egypt : Extinct city)—Exhibitions.
3. Nefertari, Queen, consort of Rameses II. King of Egypt—Tomb—
Exhibitions.    I. J. Paul Getty Museum.    II. Getty Conservation
Institute.
ND2865.T46I5   1992
751.6'2'09623—dc20                          92-20744
                                             CIP
                                             r92

Photo Credits: Guillermo Aldana, figs. 1, 2, 4, 8–17, 30, 34–36, 38, cover,
endsheets, title page, copyright page, table of contents; Archives of Late Egyp-
tian Art, Robert S. Bianchi, New York, figs. 18, 20, 22–27, 31–33, 37; Cleveland
Museum of Art, fig. 29; Image processing by Earthsat, fig. 7; Metropolitan
Museum of Art, New York, figs. 6, 19, 28; Museo Egizio, Turin, figs. 5, 21 (Lovera
Giacomo, photographer), half-title page.

Cover: Queen Nefertari. Chamber C, south wall (detail), before treatment was
completed. Endsheets: Ceiling pattern, yellow five-pointed stars on dark blue
ground. Half-title page: Stereo view of tomb entrance taken by Don Michele
Piccio/Francesco Ballerini, circa 1904. Title page: View of Chamber K, looking
north. Copyright page: Chamber C, south wall, after final treatment. Table of
Contents page: Chamber C, south wall (detail), after final treatment. Tomb of
Nefertari, Western Thebes, Egypt.

Published on the occasion of an exhibition at the J. Paul Getty Museum, Malibu,
November 12, 1992–February 21, 1993. The exhibition was organized by the
Museum in cooperation with The Getty Conservation Institute.

# Contents

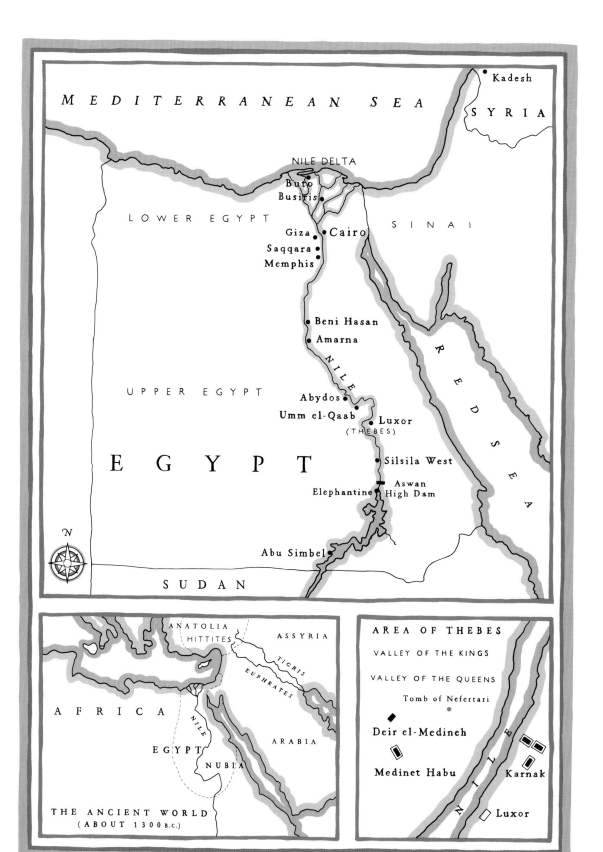

MEDITERRANEAN SEA

SYRIA

Kadesh

NILE DELTA

Buto
Busiris

LOWER EGYPT

SINAI

Giza
Cairo
Saqqara
Memphis

Beni Hasan

Amarna

UPPER EGYPT

NILE

Abydos
Umm el-Qaab
Luxor
(THEBES)

EGYPT

Silsila West

Elephantine
Aswan
High Dam

RED SEA

N

Abu Simbel

SUDAN

ANATOLIA
HITTITES

ASSYRIA

TIGRIS

EUPHRATES

AFRICA

NILE

ARABIA

EGYPT

NUBIA

THE ANCIENT WORLD
(ABOUT 1300 B.C.)

AREA OF THEBES

VALLEY OF THE KINGS

VALLEY OF THE QUEENS

Tomb of Nefertari

Deir el-Medineh

NILE

Medinet Habu

Karnak

Luxor

# Foreword

*In the Tomb of Nefertari: Conservation of the Wall Paintings* illustrates the joint project undertaken by the Egyptian Antiquities Organization (EAO) and the Getty Conservation Institute (GCI) to rescue one of the most treasured monuments of ancient Egyptian art and culture. Rameses II immortalized his favorite queen by having her resting place decorated according to the religious and artistic traditions of the time. Some thirty-two hundred years later, an international group of experts called upon the best scientific traditions of our own age to help sustain that initial intent. In this joint effort, we have bridged the gap that separates us from our past and distinguishes us from one another in the present. We have attempted a monumental effort founded on the assumptions that the arts give us spiritual enrichment and that they offer a category of experience that binds us together as a multicultural community of men and women.

The wall paintings of the Tomb of Nefertari suffered damage during ancient times and had deteriorated extensively since the tomb's discovery in 1904. In 1985 the GCI proposed to join forces with the EAO to rescue them. The GCI's proposal outlined an approach to existing problems rarely encountered in the course of the EAO's diverse collaborative efforts in the field of archaeological conservation in the past. The GCI's laudable conservation philosophy, the soundness of their scientific approach, and their promise to put the most competent conser-

vators to work led to the EAO's decision to endorse the proposal. Today the sad fate that once awaited the tomb has been transformed into a cause for festive celebration. Our debt of gratitude to the GCI is inestimable. Egypt has regained a singular representation of her cultural heritage. A further gain is the number of Egyptian candidates who received hands-on training in wall painting conservation. In a land with as demanding and fragile a cultural landscape as Egypt, the value of human resources with conservation expertise and experience is too obvious to require comment.

We are grateful to the J. Paul Getty Museum for mounting an exhibition devoted to enhancing public awareness of the conservation problems of the Tomb of Nefertari. The exhibition is a commentary on the measure of specialized skills, and particularly the level of general education, required to perpetuate the life of this and similar monuments in the future. It is hoped that comparable activities will be undertaken and multiplied elsewhere in the world. We have to realize that the custodianship of our artistic heritage is the privilege and responsibility not only of specialized organizations, conservation professionals, scholars, and scientists but of people everywhere.

Mohamed Ibrahim Bakr
Chairman
Egyptian Antiquities Organization

# Preface

VISITORS WHO KNOW THE GETTY Museum's collections will be surprised to come upon an exhibition on an Egyptian topic in our galleries. With the exception of mummy portraits of the Roman period, we have no Egyptian material, and this is the first time Egyptian art has been shown here. This is also our first exhibition about the conservation of a work of art still in situ. We had never had the possibility of documenting the treatment of a major monument until our colleagues at the Getty Conservation Institute undertook the effort to save the Tomb of Nefertari.

In their powerful design, sure line, fresh color, and inventive compositions, the paintings in this tomb rival the best of later European art. But few people have seen them, since the tomb was closed for decades to all but specialists. Now, thanks to the team assembled by the GCI and headed by Paolo and Laura Mora, the paintings not only have been preserved for the future but also have been cleaned to reveal the astonishing brilliance of their original appearance.

We are grateful to the many American museums that lent us objects associated with Nefertari and her tomb. Dorothea Arnold, Curator of Egyptian Art, Metropolitan Museum of Art, New York; Robert Bianchi, formerly Associate Curator of Egyptian Art, Brooklyn Museum (now J. Clawson Mills Fellow, Metropolitan Museum of Art, New York); Rita Freed, Curator of Egyptian Art, Museum of Fine Arts, Boston;

Arielle Kozloff, Curator of Ancient Art, Cleveland Museum of Art; Gerry Scott III, Curator of Ancient Art, San Antonio Museum Association; and Nancy Thomas, Associate Curator of Ancient and Islamic Art, Los Angeles County Museum of Art, all were generous with their expertise as well as their collections. We owe particular thanks to Dr. W. Benson Harer, San Bernardino, for the loan of his statue of Nefertari, and to the staff of the Museo Egizio, Turin, for allowing us to reproduce photographs of Ernesto Schiaparelli's original excavation of the tomb from their unique collection of glass negatives.

Our greatest debt is to our colleagues at the GCI under the leadership of Director Miguel Angel Corzo, as well as to the team of conservators whose work has given us the opportunity for this exhibition. We are proud to be able to provide a showcase for their remarkable achievements. We are grateful to Harold M. Williams, President and Chief Executive Officer, J. Paul Getty Trust, for his steadfast support of an exhibition that proved more complex than expected.

It was in 1989, after her first visit to the Tomb of Nefertari with Luis Monreal, then director of the GCI, that Marion True, Curator of Antiquities, proposed this exhibition. Deborah Gribbon, Associate Director and Chief Curator, helped develop the idea for the show and coordinated the collaboration between the Museum and the GCI. Karen Manchester, Associate Curator of Antiquities,

supervised the plans for installation and
the making of the replica of one of the
tomb chambers. Bruce Metro and the
Preparations staff at the Museum assisted
with the construction of the replica, the
tomb model, and the installation furniture. Jerry Podany and the staff of Antiquities Conservation worked together
with the conservators of the lending
institutions to create safe and controlled
environments for the fragile objects
included in the displays. Publication
Services staff Kurt Hauser and Elizabeth
Burke Kahn were responsible for the
design and production of this publication. Charles Passela, Head of Photographic Services, advised regarding the
chamber replica, and Barbara Anderson,
Collections Projects Administrator,
coordinated all aspects of the exhibition.

John Walsh
Director
J. Paul Getty Museum

# Introduction

In September 1985 the Egyptian Antiquities Organization and the Getty Conservation Institute agreed to undertake a joint project for the conservation of the wall paintings of the Tomb of Nefertari. Seven years later, the damages inflicted by time, nature, and humankind have been arrested, and the surviving paintings have regained their original grace. Yet in spite of all the painstaking work, their condition remains vulnerable. These paintings stand as testimony to the creative genius of ancient Egyptian artists and as a celebration of art by an international community of policymakers and conservation professionals. The paintings' survival will depend largely on the protection they receive in the years that lie ahead. The present exhibition on the Joint EAO-GCI Nefertari Conservation Project is designed as a tribute to the artist's skill, but mainly to the conservator's craft. It is also meant to generate a broader awareness of the conservation problems of cultural property which should rightly be a public concern.

The basic premise of our conservation philosophy at the GCI is that cultural property warrants preservation not only because of its intrinsic value as art—a source of aesthetic expression and experience—but also because of its extrinsic value as a document encoding data about human history and civilization. Cultural property is a record of our human condition on both a spiritual and a material plane. To decipher it is to know our past. To preserve it is to pass that knowledge on to future generations.

Translated into policy and practice, this essentially humanistic approach means that we apply nonintrusive techniques and reversible conservation materials to damaged works of art in order not to disturb the authenticity of the data. We conserve and stabilize, but do not add or reconstruct. In the case of the Tomb of Nefertari, for instance, the gaps and areas that had suffered paint loss—whether large or small—were covered with mud-plaster specially prepared from local materials and textured in a fashion aesthetically compatible with the tomb's environment. We believe that the tomb's architectural space, coupled with the quality and extent of the surviving wall paintings, is generous enough—despite the many missing parts—to allow for an inner, mental reconstruction of the representations into an integral whole.

By all accounts, the wall paintings are among the most exquisite in ancient Egyptian art. This superior status and the equally formidable challenges offered by their conservation were the main reasons why we first decided to undertake the project. When Paolo and Laura Mora accepted our invitation to assemble and direct the conservation team, we felt hopeful that the task could actually be done. The pictures in this exhibition speak for themselves. The public will be the judge of the team's collective achievement. Our mission will be accomplished when individuals everywhere, better educated in deterioration processes and conservation principles, acknowledge that until longer-term solutions to the problems of decay are found, these and similarly rare and delicate works of art comprise an endangered species. That species needs to be safeguarded from the risks of unrestrained exposure to visitors. The Getty Museum's initiative in organizing an exhibition aimed at raising the level of public awareness on conservation issues is itself a significant sign that our mission is not an illusory one. It adds yet another dimension to a complex network of integrative conservation activities involving specialized experience in scientific inquiry, wall painting conservation, artistic sensitivity, and appropriate policy decisions and management strategies.

We are grateful to Mohamed Ibrahim Bakr, Chairman, Egyptian Antiquities Organization, and to his predecessors Sayed Tawfik, Ahmed Kadry, and Gamal Moukhtar, who endorsed the project and facilitated our task with their trust and good will. Frank Preusser, Associate Director, Programs, GCI, contributed his vast scientific expertise to the project. Eduardo Porta, the project's field coordinator, deserves special mention. We are greatly indebted to Romany Helmy, the project field agent, who gave us the benefit of his inexhaustible stamina, intelligent planning, and excellent humor over several difficult years.

Paolo and Laura Mora are, of course, a category unto themselves, and we thank and honor them for the superior quality of their work and diligence. Our heartfelt thanks go to the individual members of the conservation team who worked so hard to keep Nefertari alive, to Guillermo Aldana, who captured their excellent work in thousands of now historic photographs, and to Mahasti Afshar, Program Research Associate, GCI, who helped to develop the exhibition in collaboration with the Museum and who authored the panel texts describing the project.

An international team of scientists has contributed its critical knowledge to a better understanding of the tomb's deterioration problems. We acknowledge our indebtedness to them collectively. We are presently conducting research on issues of site protection. Shin Maekawa, Head, Environmental Sciences, GCI, has designed and implemented a monitoring system to collect data on environmental factors affecting the tomb paintings. These data will be used to determine the number and frequency of visitors which might be considered safe. Neville Agnew, Special Projects Director, GCI, will continue to supervise the final phase of monitoring and site protection.

Miguel Angel Corzo
Director
The Getty Conservation Institute

**FIGURE I**
View across the Nile
toward Western Thebes.

# The Conservation
## of the Wall Paintings

*F*rom very early times, the ancient Egyptians imagined that the dead inhabited a land west of the Nile River (see map), where they lived in a fashion not so different from that of the living. The actual journey to the netherworld involved a dangerous nighttime passage that began in the west and imitated the course of the sun between its setting and rising. Access to eternal life depended on the punctilious observance by the living of funerary customs and rituals that had evolved over the course of centuries. These beliefs were so strong that the ancient Egyptians sited their cemeteries west of the river whenever possible, placing them not in cultivated areas, but on the edge of the desert or in the canyons leading down to the river valley.

Western Thebes was the preferred site for the burial of kings and queens during the New Kingdom. There were two royal cemeteries, each located in a valley cutting down through limestone hills. Today these are known as the Valley of the Kings and Valley of the Queens, respectively. To reach them, one has first to cross the Nile from modern Luxor (fig. 1) and then traverse a broad band of richly tilled fields. Beyond these, about two kilometers from the river and at the limit of the cultivation, is the soaring pylon of Medinet Habu, the great temple

of the pharaoh Rameses III. This is the largest in a phalanx of royal mortuary palaces which ranges north along the desert margin. Forming a backdrop to these sprawling edifices are the low hills of Sheikh Abd-el-Qurna and Qurna Murai, which are honeycombed with the tombs of over four hundred Theban nobles. The remains of the community of ancient workmen who excavated and decorated the royal tombs are set in a shallow depression just over a rise southwest of Qurna Murai. The royal necropolises themselves lie farther west, hidden in the desert canyons.

The Valley of the Queens (fig. 2) is formed by two rock spurs that jut out from the large mountain mass called El-Qurn, a prominent peak that can be seen from just about anywhere in Luxor. Over the eons, wind and water have eroded the flanks of the valley to create a natural amphitheater that slopes from northwest to southeast, issuing not far from Medinet Habu. Although called *ta set neferu* by the ancient Egyptians, it is known in Arabic as either Biban el-Harim or Biban el-Malikat, variously translated as "Portals of the Ladies" or—preferably—"Portals of the Queens." "Portals" is probably a reference to the tomb entrances that may have been visible even before modern excavations were carried out.

As early as the late seventeenth dynasty, the valley was used occasionally as a cemetery. But by the reign of the pharaoh Tuthmosis I, it had become a site of regular interment, and during the nineteenth and twentieth dynasties it was used as a burial ground not just for queens but for princesses and princes.

**FIGURE 2**

The Valley of the Queens looking north. The entrance to the Tomb of Nefertari is visible in the middle foreground.

Indeed, its principal function may have been for the burial of royal offspring, and so its conventional designation as the Valley of the Queens is somewhat misleading. Overall, the valley contains about ninety rock-cut tombs and an assortment of simpler graves and pits.

The valley was visited in 1828–29 by Jean-François Champollion, the decipherer of ancient Egyptian hieroglyphs; in 1834 by the Italian archaeologist Ippolito Rosellini; and in 1845 by Karl Richard Lepsius, who produced a massive survey of Egyptian monuments sponsored by Wilhelm IV of Prussia. But systematic exploration of this archaeologically rich area did not commence until 1904, when, under the direction of Ernesto Schiaparelli, curator of Egyptian antiquities in Turin, the Missione Archeologica Italiana in Egitto examined the site. Among the mission's discoveries was the Tomb of Nefertari, great royal wife of the pharaoh Rameses II (also known as Rameses the Great), who probably died in her forties, sometime in her husband's twenty-fourth regnal year. Although the tomb had been robbed in ancient times, Schiaparelli managed to recover a few objects that had eluded its violators. These included bits of a small chest belonging to the queen, fragments of nearly thirty *ushabti* figurines representing her, a *djed* amulet emulating the pillar associated with Osiris and the town of Busiris (a site in the Nile delta sacred to the god), a knob from a chest bearing the coronation name taken by the pharaoh Ay after he succeeded the pharaoh Tutankhamun to the throne (fig. 21), odd bits of rope and cloth, a putative scrap of the queen's

## DYNASTIES OF ANCIENT EGYPT

| | |
|---|---|
| Late Predynastic Period | circa 3000 B.C. |
| Early Dynastic Period | |
| (First–Third dynasties) | 2920–2575 |
| Old Kingdom | |
| (Fourth–Eighth dynasties) | 2575–2134 |
| First Intermediate Period | |
| (Ninth–Eleventh dynasties) | 2134–2040 |
| Middle Kingdom | |
| (Eleventh–Thirteenth dynasties) | 2040–1640 |
| Second Intermediate Period | |
| (Fourteenth–Seventeenth dynasties) | 1640–1532 |
| New Kingdom | |
| Eighteenth Dynasty | |
| Ahmose | *1550–1525 |
| Amenhotep I | 1525–1504 |
| Tuthmosis I | 1504–1492 |
| Tuthmosis II | 1492–1479 |
| Tuthmosis III | 1479–1425 |
| Hatshepsut | 1473–1458 |
| Amenhotep II | 1427–1401 |
| Tuthmosis IV | 1401–1391 |
| Amenhotep III | 1391–1353 |
| Amenhotep IV/Akhenaten | 1353–1335 |
| Smenkhkare | 1335–1333 |
| Tutankhamun | 1333–1323 |
| Ay | 1323–1319 |
| Horemheb | 1319–1307 |
| Nineteenth Dynasty | |
| Rameses I | 1307–1306 |
| Sety I | 1306–1290 |
| Rameses II | 1290–1224 |
| Merneptah | 1224–1214 |
| Sety II | 1214–1204 |
| Siptah | 1204–1198 |
| Twosre | 1198–1196 |
| Twentieth Dynasty | 1196–1070 |
| Third Intermediate Period | |
| (Twenty-first–Twenty-fourth dynasties) | 1070–712 |
| Late Period | |
| (Twenty-fifth–Thirty-first dynasties) | 712–332 |
| Macedonian–Ptolemaic Period | 332–30 B.C. |
| Roman Period | 30 B.C.–A.D. 395 |

*Dates given for individuals represent regnal period.

Adapted from John Baines and Jaromír Málek, *Atlas of Ancient Egypt* (Oxford, 1980), pp. 36–37.

mummy, and pieces of her rose granite sarcophagus lid. (All of these items are preserved in the Museo Egizio, Turin.)

Although Nefertari is depicted in a variety of monuments in Egypt and Nubia—most notably, in the rock shrine dedicated to her and the goddess Hathor at Abu Simbel—it is primarily by her tomb in the Valley of the Queens that she is known. The tomb layout is the most ambitious one there. It has a longitudinal plan, typical of late New Kingdom royal burials (earlier royal tombs tend to have a sharp, right-angled bend) and is

oriented to the north (fig. 3). Hewn out of the side of the canyon and proceeding for a distance of about 4.6 meters is a combination double stairway and ramp, down which such heavy funerary furniture as the queen's stone sarcophagus would have been lowered. This ends in an offering hall (Chamber C) with a built-in bench along three sides. On the same level, off to the right and at right angles to the tomb axis, is a suite of rooms (Chambers D through G). Issuing from the offering hall is a second descent about 6.1 meters long—

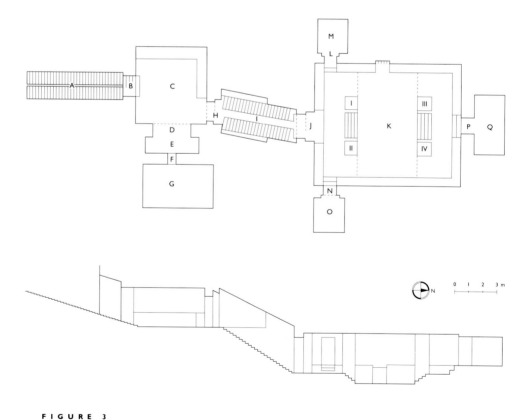

**FIGURE 3**

Plan and elevation of Nefertari's tomb.

again a ramp superimposed on a flight of stairs—that ends in a sarcophagus chamber (K) supported by four squared pillars that are part of the original rock mass. This burial hall is approximately rectangular, with its longest dimension running north–south. The queen's sarcophagus would have been positioned here, with its head end to the west. Finally, three small chambers, one each to the east, west, and north, lead off the burial hall.

Like most of the royal and private tombs in Western Thebes, Nefertari's has suffered as a result of the poor quality of the local limestone. Unlike the limestone at Giza and Saqqara to the north—which permitted the carving of high-quality reliefs—the rock in Western Thebes has been fractured, through either seismic activity or the upwelling of shale deposits beneath the limestone. In Nefertari's tomb the ancient masons were not able to produce smooth, firm rock surfaces suitable for carving or painting. Instead, they had to apply a plaster underlay, followed by a coat of fine plaster. Only then could the walls receive preliminary draftsmen's sketches and final drawings. The hieroglyphic texts and vignettes making up the decorative scheme of the tomb were modeled in the plaster and painted in vibrant red, yellow, green, and blue, contrasted against white backgrounds and jet black outlines. More than 520 square meters of wall surface in a half-dozen chambers and vestibules were thus embellished with the story of Nefertari's final journey from life through death and into immortality via a secret realm of gates and caverns (fig. 4). In doing this, the anonymous artisans of ancient Thebes wrought

one of the finest painted tombs of the Pharaonic period.

In 1905, once Schiaparelli had finished his work in the Tomb of Nefertari, it was opened to the public. From the outset, scholarly and public praise for the tomb's superbly decorated walls was tempered by the knowledge that the paintings and their plaster supports had suffered terribly over the centuries. More

FIGURE 4

Chamber G, west wall: Nefertari crowned with the vulture headdress of Nekhbet, the protective goddess of Upper Egypt.

**FIGURE 5**

A comparison of this archival photograph, taken by Schiaparelli and his team circa 1904, with the one illustrated in figure 6 shows graphically the tomb's progressive deterioration over a period of approximately fifteen years.

worrisome was the fact—apparent through observation and from accumulating photographic evidence—that the tomb was *still* deteriorating, largely as a result of the carelessness of visitors but also because of inherent weaknesses in the wall paintings. Appreciating the risks involved in keeping the tomb open, the Egyptian authorities closed it in 1934, and so it has remained.

In the eighty-eight years that have passed since the tomb's discovery, it has been meticulously observed and repeatedly photographed. These historic photographs, which now number in the thousands, are essential for documenting and understanding its conservation problems. Selected comparisons of these views, many taken years and even decades apart, help to substantiate

ongoing paint and plaster loss (figs. 5, 6). The most important of these sources, one that has served as the basis for all historic studies of the tomb, is a set of 132 glass negatives shot between 1904 and 1905 by Schiaparelli and the Italian mission. To these may be added two views taken in the upper suite of rooms (Chambers E and G) in 1909 by Colin Campbell, a Scottish minister and amateur Egyptologist, as well as a series of touristic views commissioned in the 1910s by the firm of Gaddis and Seif for sale in its shops in Cairo and Luxor.

Between 1914 and 1916, Robert Mond, a British Egyptologist, completed a thorough photographic mosaic of Chamber G, which contains some of the most memorable scenes in the entire tomb, especially the view of the gods

FIGURE 6
Photograph taken by Harry Burton circa 1920–1923, showing the same scene reproduced in figure 5.

Osiris and Atum enthroned back to back before altars heaped with offerings. The consistency of scale and focus of Mond's shots makes them an unusually reliable resource for monitoring the condition of the murals in that area of the tomb. A few years later, beginning in 1920 and concluding about 1923, the Metropolitan Museum of Art, New York, sent its photographer Harry Burton throughout Egypt to survey monuments. The results of that trip include over sixty shots of Nefertari's tomb.

The Documentation Center of the Egyptian Antiquities Organization (EAO), located on the island of Zamalek in Cairo, carried out perhaps the most exhaustive photographic program. Conducted in two phases by Ghazouli and X. F. Ibrahim in 1958 and 1965,

respectively, it produced a huge archive of black and white images which, although not published, may be consulted. The earliest color views of the tombs to survive were taken in 1953 by Claudio Emmer for Arpag Mekhitarian's book *La Peinture égyptienne*. The three shots, all of the upper suite, show Nefertari variously playing the game of *senet*, offering linen to the god Ptah, and adoring seven divine cows. From a color campaign during the 1950s and 1960s, 155 shots were culled for Gertrud Thausing and Hans Goedicke's volume *Nofretari*.

The tomb's rarity and exceptional importance, coupled with worldwide concern for its well-being, made it the focus not just of Egyptian but of international committees and study groups. The reports issued by these groups complement the photo surveys by variously identifying the primary causes of decay while making general recommendations for the tomb's rehabilitation. One of the earliest, included in the 1940 annual of the Egyptian Antiquities Service (the predecessor organization to the EAO), noted that the paintings in the Tomb of Nefertari had sensibly deteriorated since 1904. The blame was put squarely (but erroneously) on the hygroscopic nature of the materials used in the tomb: the ancient plaster and paint soak up moisture. The 1940 study prescribed injections of fixatives to bond rock and plaster layers, as well as temporary removal and rebacking of severely damaged scenes. Not surprisingly, it also recommended periodic examination of the tomb and continual monitoring of temperature and humidity levels.

A report issued in May 1970 by the United Nations Educational, Scientific, and Cultural Organization (UNESCO) attributed the damage of the paintings to the effects of rain, soluble salts, and dehydration of plaster. The report urged treatments "mainly to improve adhesion of plaster to the walls, and re-enforce its cohesion strength." The International Centre for the Study of Preservation and Restoration of Cultural Property (ICCROM) survey of July 1978 emphasized the *process* of decay rather than its agents: "slow evaporation of salt-laden water with growth of salt crystals and progressive dehydration of the gypsum-based plaster, especially during long, dry periods in the tomb." The ICCROM report strongly discouraged any attempt to remove the paintings or to isolate them from the walls by means of a

separation cavity. An unpublished 1980 study issued by Cairo University focused on site protection; stabilization of the tomb's microclimate through landscaping and the fitting of a double air-tight door were among its recommendations.

The most radical proposal for protecting the murals appeared in a paper published in Warsaw in 1973 by the State Ateliers for the Preservation of Historical Property. Based on the assumption that the plaster was inherently weak and unable to support the paintings indefinitely, it concluded that "the only practicable form of conservation . . . is transference of the paintings onto new supports." Lastly, a Canadian report issued in May 1981 underscored the fragility of the microclimate, finding that even limited numbers of visitors to the tomb skewed moisture levels. It was these changes, coupled with changes in temperature, that proved so pernicious. The Canadians' recommendation was to limit public access.

Most of these studies identified the harmful agents as water and salts and were substantially in agreement on the dynamic interaction of the two. There was also strong support for some sort of intervention, but no consensus regarding specific remedies.

The decision to rehabilitate the Tomb of Nefertari, conceived jointly by the EAO and the Getty Conservation Institute (GCI) in September 1985, turned on a number of considerations. The chief concern was that an irreplaceable work of utmost importance to world culture was slipping from the cultural record. If something was not done, the only souvenirs of it might one day be a few hundred photographs and some line drawings. The joint conservation effort was announced in Cairo on September 8, 1986. Speaking for the EAO, which is responsible for all museums, monuments, and archaeological sites in Egypt, Ahmed Kadry, its chairman, highlighted the scope of collaboration required when he said that

> the EAO has been aware of the problems of the tomb for many years and has considered several approaches to its conservation. The project with the Getty Conservation Institute is our first attempt to completely study the tomb's environment and contents so that a comprehensive program for conserving the wall paintings can be determined. Not only will it benefit the Nefertari Tomb, which many consider to be the most beautiful of the Pharaonic period, but the results of our work there will facilitate the treatment of other tombs on the West Bank of the Nile that have similar problems.

Luis Monreal, then director of the GCI, and Kadry agreed to conduct a year of surveys and tests to discover the causes of decay. This was the first comprehensive scientific analysis of its kind. The scientists examined the geology of the valley, looked for evidence of water-drainage patterns, considered the effects of temperature and humidity fluctuations on the site, searched for evidence of microscopic and macroscopic plant and animal life in the tomb, and tested all materials—especially plasters, pigments, and salts—using chemical, spectrographic, and X-ray diffraction methods. Exact hues in the tomb were measured at over 160 locations using a colorimeter,

to establish baseline readings against which future deterioration could be measured. Extensive record photography was done before, during, and after all work.

While these tests were being carried out, an emergency program to consolidate the most endangered areas of the tomb was being designed by Paolo Mora and Laura Mora, the renowned wall painting conservators formerly associated with the Istituto Centrale del Restauro, Rome. Both of the Moras had spent over forty years restoring wall paintings worldwide and had had a longstanding professional interest in the Tomb of Nefertari. Their philosophy of minimal intervention, thoroughly consistent with GCI goals, reflected concern within the conservation community regarding reversibility of methods and minimal intrusion.

A multidisciplinary team of specialists invited from seven nations assembled in Cairo for the first project briefing immediately following the public announcement of the campaign to save the tomb. In addition to the Moras, the group included Hideo Arai, a biologist from the Tokyo National Research Institute of Cultural Property; Farouk el-Baz, an Egyptian geologist and director of the Center for Remote Sensing, Boston University; Modesto Montoto, a petrologist from the University of Oviedo, Spain; and Guillermo Aldana, a Mexican photographer with wide experience in archaeological work. Feisal Esmael, who acted as scientific adviser to the EAO, proposed to do a survey of the tomb's internal climate. Also serving as advisers were two of Egypt's most respected Egyptologists: Gamal Moukhtar, former chairman of the EAO, and Gaballa A. Gaballa, vice dean of the Faculty of Archaeology at Cairo University.

Representing the GCI along with Luis Monreal was Miguel Angel Corzo. Corzo, named director of the GCI in January 1991, was then director of Special Projects. He developed the project, assembled the experts and the required equipment, and insured ongoing logistical support. Also from the GCI were Frank Preusser and, assisting him, Michael Schilling, Associate Scientist. As director of the Scientific Program at the GCI, Preusser had overall responsibility for designing and interpreting the battery of tests on which conservation measures were to be based.

As Corzo observed on that day in 1986, superficially the team was more remarkable for its breadth of disciplines,

cultures, languages, and personalities than for any conceivable common purpose. But surveys began at once, and the group quickly found itself functioning as a unit. Hideo Arai, an expert on biodeterioration of cultural monuments and the first member of the team to enter the tomb, established a baseline for bacterial activity by taking samples of the air inside. A second sampling done three days later, after just six people had entered the tomb, showed that bacterial counts had risen 300 percent. Arai's data, coupled with evidence assembled later that relative humidity around or above 70 percent could trigger bacterial growth and biologic activity in the tomb, was to be important as debate regarding public access unfolded. Farouk el-Baz reconstructed water-flow patterns in the valley through the use of topographic maps generated by laser technology and the analysis of infrared photographs taken by a Landsat-5 satellite (fig. 7). He demonstrated that periodic deluges affected the Valley of the Queens only once or twice a century.

Additional surveys of microflora, measurements of color, experiments in nondestructive testing methods, and materials analyses went on over a period of a year. A thorough review of the site's history and documentation as well as condition surveys charting the complex interdynamics of rock, plaster, pigment, salt, and water were carried out. The results gained from this welter of tests and archival screenings helped frame the specific treatments—both short- and long-term—that eventually were put into effect. As a result of these tests, a full and dynamic picture of the course of

**FIGURE 7**

An infrared view of the Luxor area taken by a Landsat-5 satellite. Visible are the desert plateau to the west and the system of wadis that lead down into the Nile River valley. The arrow indicates the vicinity of Nefertari's tomb.

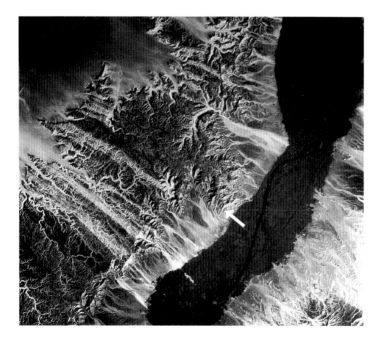

FIGURE 8

Close-up view of a salt vein showing massive crystals as they pry the painted surface away from the plaster.

deterioration could be drawn.

The limestone bed into which the Tomb of Nefertari was cut shows a network of large and small fissures, probably due to seismic activity. Over the course of tens of millennia, soluble salts of nearly pure sodium chloride (gypsum in some strata) have washed into the fissures, building up an inexhaustible reservoir impossible to extract from the rock or the wall paintings (which are water soluble).

Water, whether liquid or vapor, is the catalyst activating the salts; it dissolves them. As it evaporates, crystals, fibers, and needles of salt form slowly, either in the voids within or between layers of materials or on the painted surfaces. The larger crystals are very hard and interpose themselves between rock and plaster or plaster and paint (fig. 8). The expanding crystal lattices exert an irresistible pressure that pries the structure of plaster and paint apart. Salt encrustations on the painted surfaces erode the paint itself, leaving the colors blistered and chalky, so that they can be wiped away by a careless touch.

There are three ways in which water can enter the tomb, and in all likelihood, each has been responsible for part of the damage. First of all, when the ancient Egyptians plastered and painted the tomb, they were required to use large amounts of water, thus activating salts already present within the rock. Secondly, recent archaeological work has uncovered accumulations of water-deposited sediment in the Valley of the Queens. This is interpreted as evidence of torrential rains, probably in the Late Period and Roman era. Rainwater flowing through cracks in the rock strata or coursing down the mouth of the tomb could have reached the wall paintings as either liquid or vapor. (Schiaparelli did report traces of dried puddles in Nefertari's burial hall, Chamber K, although the damage observable around the base of that hall, the tomb's lowest point [fig. 9], was not caused by standing water.) The situation is far different in the Valley

**FIGURE 9**

Delamination of plaster on the northeast side of Chamber K.

of the Kings, where the tomb of Rameses II, Nefertari's husband, contains between 2.1 and 2.4 meters of stratified, water-laid sediments. The sole evidence for the *percolation* of liquid water into Nefertari's tomb is the presence of two water spots high on the front left wall in Chamber C and not far from an ancient fault in the stone. Veins in the stone matrix may be too tightly packed with salt to even allow the passage of liquid water.

The third source of water in the tomb is vapor present in the surrounding air. When the relative humidity exceeds certain levels—either because liquid water has entered the tomb or because there are excessive numbers of visitors—the salts start taking up water, forming a saturated solution. Although pure sodium chloride crystals start to take up water when relative humidity levels exceed about 75 percent, complex mixtures, such as mud-plaster with salt or mud-plaster with gypsum and salt, and different forms of salt can absorb moisture at much lower levels, even as low as 50 percent.

Apart from the action of salts, the composition of the plaster has raised concerns. Made of gypsum mixed with sand, clay, and chopped straw, it may have dehydrated completely over the centuries, resulting in its shrinking and peeling away from the rock support.

Vibration resulting from tourist bus traffic may have contributed minutely to damage in the past. However, the Centre National de Recherche Scientifique, Paris, which has worked in the Valley of the Queens for two decades, has shortened by several hundred meters the macadam roadway tourist buses must take to the site. With passengers disembarking further away, the threat of vibration has been removed.

An understanding of these destructive processes coupled with an awareness of the other stresses on the tomb—old fixatives, repaintings (figs. 10, 11), refacings, relinings, repositionings, physical damage from visitors, and a great deal of dust and dirt everywhere—barely conveys the shock of seeing so much beauty despoiled. But an imaginary tour

**FIGURES 10, 11**
One of the aesthetic dilemmas faced by the conservators: to retain or remove old inpainting. The south wall of Chamber G, showing eight celestial cows, was touched up by Schiaparelli, as the infrared view in figure 10 shows. In this case, the inpainting was retained (fig. 11) while in other areas it was covered with removable textured plaster to signal that the original decorated surface had been lost.

FIGURE 12

A good deal of the decorated surface of the west wall of Chamber C has been lost.

through the Tomb of Nefertari just prior to the commencement of work by the EAO-GCI team can accomplish this.

Moving down the descent into the tomb, one passes from intense light and heat into deep shade and near-total darkness. The atmosphere is close and still; nothing stirs, not even the faintest hint of a breeze. Surprisingly the tomb seems cool, even though it is summer outside.

In the first chamber there is a built-in bench along the left-hand wall. A heron and two funerary goddesses, Nephthys and Isis, appear in a frieze at the top of the wall. A great deal of paint and plaster has fallen away. Scratches and abrasions are observable, and much text and imagery have been lost in this scene. By a quick estimate, perhaps a third of the decoration seems to have vanished (fig. 12). In an antechamber to the right is a figure of the queen herself being conducted by the hawk-headed god Horus-son-of-Isis (Horsiese) into the presence of another god, Rehorakhty, also hawk-headed but wearing the uraeus serpent and solar disk. The queen's dress and the lower portion of the scene in particular are disfigured with black spotting. The throne on which Rehorakhty sits is covered with a red and green feather pattern, but part of it looks as if it has been repainted. Salt blooms leaching out through the paint appear as small, crusty patches; wherever they occur, the colors look chalky. Deeper into the chamber, above a once splendid scene of enthroned gods, is a huge bulge of plaster. Like an enormous blister, it could break at any time and shower plaster down onto the tomb floor.

The corridor that descends to the burial chamber once had dozens of vertical columns of brightly painted hieroglyphs; now the colors can scarcely be made out beneath a shroud of dust and dirt. In the burial chamber itself, large salt crystals resembling miniature cityscapes peep out from behind portions of plaster. They are hard and push the plaster right off the wall. Around the base, the process has gone so far that slabs of plaster—some six or seven centimeters thick—have actually sheeted off, carrying away paint and exposing the limestone behind them, which appears rough and salt-encrusted. The ceiling of the tomb, spangled with yellow five-pointed stars on a blue ground, is blistered and in danger of flaking away. At some point in the past, sheets of gauze or fabric were glued onto one extensive scene. Elsewhere mortar or cement has been puddled into cracks and fissures and around fragments, sometimes spilling over onto the painted designs. A few insects' nests and cobwebs hang in corners. There are even some insect carapaces littering the floor. It is very beautiful and also quite sad.

The stages of decay in the Tomb of Nefertari were extremely varied. A precise plot of the exact location and nature of damage throughout the tomb had to be on file and available to each conservator before he or she would dare to wield a scalpel or cotton swab anywhere. The Moras and their team spent three months compiling over two hundred condition surveys showing alterations to the support medium, alterations of the paint, the type and location of foreign substances, and a record of previous work. To begin with, the tomb was photographed at a scale of one to twenty. The photographs were then reduced as simplified line drawings. Four separate acetate maps were made, one for each type of alteration. The degree of damage was color-coded, with red signifying the most perilous state (see pp. 72–73). Within each category, the severity of decay varied greatly. Thus the status of a painting might be relatively unaffected, show superficial spotting and discoloration, have foreign matter such as dust and insect broods, show incipient chalking and flaking, or indicate abrasion and paint loss. The plaster support could be suffering from fragmentation or separation, contain extruded rock chips, and show major or minor losses. Salts were recorded in a category of their own that included minor efflorescences on paint layers and macroscopic intrusions. A final category recorded previous restoration attempts under the subheadings of retouchings, overpaintings, surface treatments, use of facings, and use of mortar to fill cracks and fissures.

It took boldness and a high degree of diplomacy and organization to implement the EAO-GCI project to begin with, but to actually do the work required a quality of nerve few of us have. Despite the total reversibility of emergency measures, the stress of presuming to work on a cultural icon of such importance was immense.

The initial survey indicated that about 20 percent of the decorated surface had already been irretrievably lost, so it was essential to protect against further losses until an appropriate conservation

**FIGURE 13**

A few of the more than ten thousand Japanese mulberry-bark paper bandages used to hold loose fragments in place during the emergency treatment process. This view shows the goddess Selkis.

strategy could be devised. Therefore, an emergency treatment plan was worked up in January 1987 and carried out between April 5 and July 5 of that year. The most serious cause of decay was loss of cohesion and adhesion in the plaster. To stop the structural disintegration of the most fragile areas and prevent their complete detachment, strips of fine-grained Japanese mulberry-bark paper were placed over any raised fragments and carefully attached using a dilute solution of acrylic resin applied at each end of the strip (fig. 13). Dangling fragments were reattached by placing a drop of the same acrylic resin emulsion on their undersides and then pushing them into their original locations using a protective sheet of silicon paper and a spatula. Because of the roughness and weight of ceiling fragments, thin strips of stronger cotton gauze were used to hold them in place temporarily. In total, approximately ten thousand protective bandages were applied to the ceiling and walls. While this was going on, further tests were conducted by the chief conservators to develop methods and materials that would be used in the actual conservation of the tomb.

In 1988, the year final treatment began, two campaigns were carried out: from January 31 to March 31, and from October 14 to December 15. Keeping in mind the rigors of the Upper Egyptian climate and the microenvironment of the tomb, no more than two annual outings were considered feasible.

In general, treatment proceeded from the inside of the tomb out, beginning with the burial chamber in 1988 and ending with the upper suite of rooms in the spring of 1992. At the start of any one campaign, each conservator was assigned a specific section or scene to work on and was supplied with a copy of the relevant reference photograph, drawn from either the Schiaparelli or the Burton archive. While this was going on, the photographer, Guillermo Aldana, began to duplicate Schiaparelli's views exactly in color and in black and white. These views and angles were shot again when the project was completed, both to show what had been achieved and to serve as a benchmark in the event of future changes within the tomb. Additionally, each step in the conservation process was documented, resulting in a collection of over five thousand slides. As field coordinator for the project (following Omar el-Arini), Eduardo Porta, professor of conservation at Barcelona University, was responsible for maintaining the daily regime, which included the keeping of logbooks by each conservator.

Initial preparation of all surfaces for

final conservation required the removal of a thick layer of dust and any vestiges of cobwebs or insect nests. Since even the most gentle direct contact with the wall posed great risk, a low-pressure air stream was directed at the surfaces. Next, sections of dense, heavy gauze that had been applied using a strong adhesive in the course of previous conservation efforts (fig. 14) were removed by brushing the surfaces with a solvent. Once dissolved, the gauze was slowly peeled away by pulling it up diagonally and flush to

FIGURE 14
Old gauzes holding plaster
in position, 1986.

the painted surface. Additional solvent was applied beneath the facing wherever needed. Some small areas that had been faced with masking tape impregnated with wax were removed too, but by using a different solvent applied with cotton.

Occasionally, the plaster layers beneath were badly disintegrated and needed immediate consolidation. This was accomplished by applying strips of tissue paper moistened with a dilute acrylic resin solution. Detached fragments of plaster and paint which had fallen between the wall and the facings or into gaps were retrieved with forceps and repositioned whenever possible. In the course of interventions predating the EAO-GCI project, many old cracks and fissures had been filled with extremely obdurate gypsum-based mortar and cement. Wherever the mortar had strayed onto decorated surfaces, its removal was slow and time-consuming. After extraneous fill had been stripped out, the delicate edges of the original material were coated with an acrylic resin to shield them from humidity introduced by the new plaster applied during conservation. The plaster used to fill in small or large losses was similar to the original, but contained varying amounts of gypsum, thus avoiding any potentially damaging tension caused by the varying expansion rates between old and new material. Mortar was applied conservatively and in thin layers that were allowed to dry thoroughly between successive applications. The new mortar surface was scored and stippled as needed so as to harmonize visually with adjacent patches of original surface.

Of all the problems facing the conser-

vation team, the reattachment and consolidation of plaster layers to the rock substrate was the most vexing. Visual inspection disclosed many areas of loss and delamination; the more difficult detection of hidden voids was achieved by gently tapping the plaster surface. (A study exploring the use of ultrasound had concluded that existing techniques were insufficiently developed to be of direct use during this phase of the project.)

To protect plaster and paint surfaces, areas to be worked on were covered where necessary with synthetic tissue affixed with an acrylic solution. To prevent the absorption of water by the extremely water-sensitive painted plaster, at first a small quantity of diluted acrylic solution was injected to form a water-impermeable seal. The mortar was composed of three parts local sand, washed to remove salts and sieved, and one part gypsum. Only as much water was added as was required to make the mortar fluid. In some instances, the amount of water was decreased to achieve a quick-drying mix. In other cases, three to five drops of acrylic resin solution were added to the mortar to slow the drying rate and prevent the absorption of moisture by the sensitive painted plaster. Any blisters sufficiently softened during the consolidation process were pressed back into position using padded tension presses sprung from a scaffold positioned in front of the surface being repaired.

Especially large voids were filled with loose stones and rock chips that were then aggregated with the mortar mix. Wherever large quantities of mortar were required, a drier mix was generally preferred to avoid risk of moisture percolating into the plaster. The protective tissues applied before consolidation were removed with solvents after these operations had been completed.

Small, partially separated fragments were hinged to the surrounding matrix, and their undersides were freed of foreign matter such as salts and rocks using scalpels and microdrills. Any disintegrated clay-straw plaster behind them was raked out. Once the fragments had been cleaned, they were impregnated with an acrylic resin solution and repositioned on a bed of drier mortar such as had been used in the consolidation process, but in proportions that would accelerate drying time and reduce moisture absorption. Forty-eight hours after replacement, the protective facings were removed.

Fully detached chunks of plaster required a thoroughly different strategy. Heavier tissue facings were applied and a molded cradle of polyurethane foam on a cane framework was fabricated to hold each fragment and allow it to be shifted safely. Once a fragment had been moved away from the wall, lightweight hammers and chisels were used to remove accumulations of dirt, salt, gypsum, and cement from previous repairs on the reverse sides and on the rock substrate itself. In some cases, as many as eight or nine inches of accumulated fill had to be laboriously chipped away. Once cleaned, the reverse of the plaster was impregnated with resin, and its thickness was built up using the mortar mixture with water and resin proportions adjusted for drying rates. The parent rock was prepared

similarly and was provided with fast-setting plaster mortar bridges on which the fragment could be safely held in place. After injections, tensioned presses held the fragment until the mortar was thoroughly set. Lastly, all protective facings were removed.

Raised or unattached flakes of paint were repositioned using acrylic resin emulsion applied to the backs of loose chips by means of a pipette or syringe. Powdery areas were also treated with an acrylic solution that bonded the paint to the plaster.

In a final operation, the wall paintings themselves were cleaned using a battery of solvents targeted for specific types of dirt: deposits of smoke and soot from lamps, the oils from human hands, staining from previous water-based conservation treatments, salt efflorescences, repaintings done during this century, and old synthetic fixatives that had darkened with age.

As the work progressed, there was great satisfaction—even joy—among the conservators, who could sense the tomb coming back to life. Their elation doubled when a bit of a gold foil armlet that had eluded the notice of ancient plunderers was found during routine clearance of the tomb in February 1988 (fig. 15). It was clearly inscribed with hieroglyphs for a woman, perhaps the queen herself, and could be included in the small inventory of objects belonging to her. The discovery was a welcome interruption, breaking the routine of seven-hour workdays. However beautiful it may be, the tomb could not easily accommodate eight or ten conservators working at one time. Even with the fresh air pumped in through

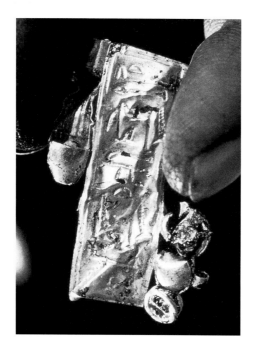

**FIGURE 15**

Bit of a gold foil armlet belonging to the queen, found behind a fragment of detached plaster in the course of cleaning the tomb in 1988.

flexible tubing attached to a small electric fan, the atmosphere was stuffy.

Despite the difficult working conditions, one of the great benefits of the Nefertari project was the training opportunities it afforded. The experience gathered over the course of eight field campaigns, complemented by a series of courses and seminars given at Luxor, proved valuable not only to the members of the Moras' team but to the seven Egyptian conservators who worked on the project as well. These Egyptian specialists are already applying the techniques perfected in the conservation of Nefertari's tomb to other damaged tombs in the Theban area.

Meanwhile, concern for the future of the Tomb of Nefertari must remain a priority. For no matter how successful the EAO-GCI conservation effort may have been, it will all have to be repeated if the environment of the tomb is not

kept under tight control. Precisely this consideration brought the technical committee of the EAO-GCI project to a meeting at Luxor in May 1989. Discussions focused on protecting and preserving the site. One of the essential conservation issues addressed was the possibility of rain- or floodwater entering the tomb. A number of strategies were put forward, ranging from careful landscaping to the installation of hidden geotextile coverings that, together with pipes, would channel water away from the site. Clearly, a master drainage scheme for the Valley of the Queens needs to be created. Flood risk—which may most prudently be dealt with by passive methods such as a raised threshold and a barrel arch to shield the entrance—was discussed. The potential impact of visitors was also considered. As we have seen, one cause of deterioration is the change in relative humidity. In this sense the tomb is like an organism; any perturbation of its environment is stressful. Since some materials in the tomb begin to absorb water when relative humidity exceeds 50 percent, and biologic activity can commence above 70 percent, the microclimate must be watched and controlled carefully, with relative humidity levels kept at or below 45 percent. The tomb is partially self-ventilating, early in the morning and again close to sunset, when the temperature inside exceeds that outside. Hot air rising out of the tomb exchanges with cooler air sinking down the sloping entrance shaft. Unfortunately, preliminary tests suggest that the tomb's atmosphere—as measured by relative humidity and carbon dioxide counts—

degrades rapidly. Its environment reacts quickly to a high number of visitors, while its capacity to recover is much slower and may even be limited.

Installation of a monitoring system has permitted the establishment of baseline data which, together with a standardized program of rephotography of selected areas at regular intervals, will help to detect any alterations early on. The types of amenities required by the public—a specially modified entrance, walkways, lighting, ventilation, and so forth—pose questions that still have to be explored in depth. Indeed, the long-term health of the tomb may not allow public access.

In the short space of six years, astonishing results have been achieved in Nefertari's tomb. What most surprises a visitor today is the subtlety of the conservation methods (fig. 16). The mortar bridges that sustain whole wall sections are out of sight; fissures have been filled and textured to blend in with surrounding surfaces; paint has been repositioned, reattached, and cleaned.

With the clockwork of repair well hidden, glittering color remains. The palette is fresh and sharp, and the designs are framed by luminous blacks and pure, almost bluish whites. Some interesting mysteries remain as well. One is the composition of some of the green

FIGURE 16

Stairway, east wall: Anubis, the jackal-headed god of embalming, guarding Nefertari's sarcophagus. Entire scenes in the tomb have been recovered by conserving, cleaning, and reintegrating the surviving portions.

pigments, which can be readily distinguished by the eye but seem to show no chemical differences. The identity of the varnish the Egyptians laid over reds and oranges to make them appear highly saturated remains elusive. The black spotting observable in some of the scenes and once thought to be caused by bacteria now appears to be a form of salt crystallization which vanishes after the thirty-second application of a damp strip of Japanese mulberry-bark paper.

But above all, the freshness of the tomb is unforgettable. The haze of dust that sat like a scrim over the paintings has been banished, allowing one to appreciate subtleties and modulations of color, line, and relief which previously went unnoticed. In the descending corridor, the queen raises a censer before the goddesses Isis and Nephthys. As the smoke curls upward, one is tempted to blow it away just to get a better look at the cones of incense in the brazier. We can even observe how Nefertari's heavy black wig was carved too broadly for the taste of the painter, who painted it more narrowly, in keeping with the queen's slender proportions. As Nefertari is led by Horsiese into the presence of the gods Rehorakhty and Hathor in the upper chamber, she blushes charmingly (fig. 17). Her diaphanous robe reveals her skin tones. The robe's hem, a fluent red line, falls in a rippling motion to the floor as the queen glides forward. On the north face of one of the columns in Chamber K, a painter brought his overfilled brush too quickly to the wall, splattering dark brown paint on the queen's cartouche and one great blob in Hathor's eye: the haste of an artisan

preserved in the solemnity of the queen's burial chamber.

In being able to appreciate fully—perhaps for the first time since the tomb was decorated—the spontaneity of the artists—their assurance and indecision, their haste and repentance—the temporal gulf that separates us from them is effectively bridged. In a demonstration of modern-day magic, the Joint EAO-GCI Nefertari Conservation Project has washed away an accumulation of years and restored the tomb, leaving us to marvel at its beauty.

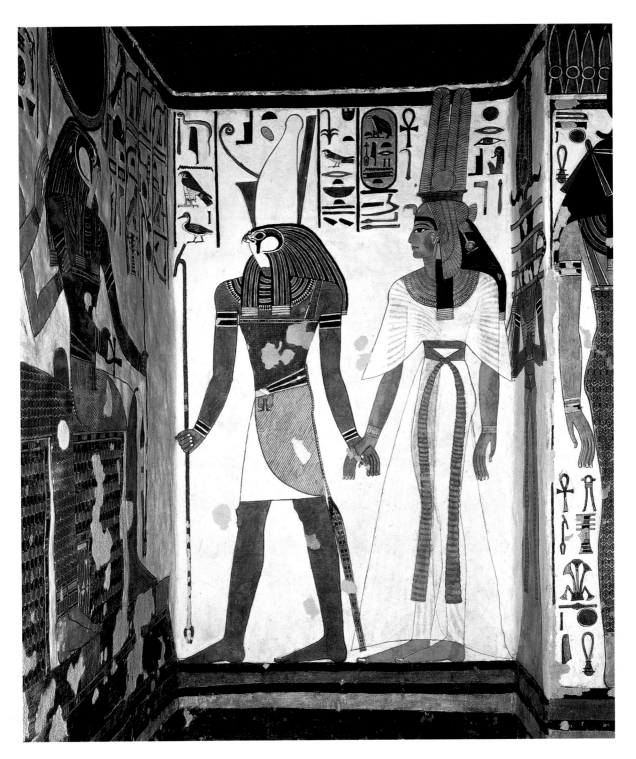

FIGURE 17

Chamber E, south wall:
Horsiese leads Nefertari
on her afterlife journey.

# Some Royal Women
of the Seventeenth and
Eighteenth Dynasties

*N efertari, for whom one of the most lavishly decorated tombs ever created in ancient Egypt was constructed, emerges from the pages of history as an important ancient Egyptian queen. In order to understand her background and the religious and political positions she occupied during the reign of her husband, Rameses the Great, the illustrious warrior-pharaoh of the nineteenth dynasty, it is advisable to pass in review the history of the New Kingdom with special*

reference to the period's royal women. Collectively, they provide many of the precedents on which Nefertari's own career was based. Some of these remarkable women were doubtless her ancestors, and a few were her sisters as well.

To do this, one must begin with the events of the seventeenth dynasty. At this time, Egypt was a divided country. The north, particularly the area of the eastern delta, was ruled by the Hyksos, a tribe whose name derived from the ancient Egyptian phrase meaning "rulers of the hill countries." These peoples had earlier invaded Egypt en masse by taking advantage of internal political dissolution at the close of the Middle Kingdom. In the south, at Elephantine, in the vicinity of the modern Aswan High Dam, the Nubians held sway, depriving the Egyptians of access to the riches of Africa beyond. The Egyptians themselves, who were confined to the area around Thebes, some five hundred kilometers south of modern Cairo, soon rallied around the banner of nationalism as a local Theban family consolidated its political position. They embarked on the so-called wars of liberation, the objective of which was to expel the Hyksos from the delta to the north and the Nubians from the south.

The historian is able to reconstruct, in broad terms, the events of those wars by relying in part on records left by the ancient Egyptians themselves. These ancient records, when studied in conjunction with evidence gleaned from archaeological excavations and other sources, indicate how the wars may have begun, how the Hyksos and Nubians may have forged an alliance against the Egyptians, and how the campaigns were waged. These battles, conducted over the course of the reigns of several Theban monarchs, culminated in the military successes of the Egyptian pharaoh Ahmose. The roles played by the queens of this period and the influence they exerted on the political and religious affairs of the day are often overlooked. It is to these women that we shall turn, specifically to Ahmose-Nefertari, the wife of the pharaoh Ahmose and the namesake of Nefertari, the wife of Rameses II.

Although direct documentation about the activities of these women does not exist, one can adduce their roles by examining Ahmose-Nefertari's career. Born of royal blood, perhaps a full or half sister of her husband, Ahmose-Nefertari appears to have maintained the tranquility of Thebes while he was away on military campaigns.

In addition to this political authority, Ahmose-Nefertari appears to have been instrumental in re-establishing in temples throughout the land the Egyptian cults that had been neglected under foreign occupation. This activity was related to a clever move on her part by which she exchanged a minor priestly office for that of the so-called "God's Wife," a rank that soon came to be associated with that of the high priestess of the Egyptian state god Amun at Thebes. The terms of this transaction are recorded on the *Donation Stela*, an inscribed commemorative stone marker on which four figures are represented (fig. 18). At the far left is Queen Ahmose-Nefertari, preceded by a smaller figure of one of her sons, perhaps to be identified as an older brother of the future pharaoh Amenhotep I. The center of the composition is occupied by a figure of the pharaoh Ahmose, who is shown making an offering to the god Amun. According to the inscriptions on this stela, Ahmose-Nefertari not only acquired religious prestige by becoming the God's Wife but also received an enormous payment consisting in part of precious metals, articles of clothing woven from the finest linen, wigs, and cosmetics. (It must be remembered that money in the modern sense had not been invented, and that wealth was acquired, accumulated, and transmitted by the exchange between parties of any number of commodities, including but not limited to those just enumerated.) By means of this same transaction, Ahmose-Nefertari also acquired title to an estate in Western Thebes as well as to the personnel to work it. The revenues generated from this new estate both contributed to the wealth of the cult of the Theban god Amun and increased the financial well-being of Ahmose-Nefertari and her successors, because she was permitted to pass the estate on to her heirs.

The acquisition of such an estate by a woman was not unusual. Women in ancient Egypt exercised rights equal to those of men regarding the conferment and transfer of property, including property acquired by inheritance or by other means both before and after marriage. In general, therefore, the status of women was more progressive than that in either ancient Greece or Rome. Since the relative scale of figures in group compositions in ancient Egyptian art is directly proportional to the corresponding importance of those represented, this equality was emphasized by the sculptors of the *Donation Stela*, on which Ahmose-Nefertari is shown as equal in stature to both her husband and the god Amun.

As the God's Wife in the capital city of Thebes, Ahmose-Nefertari consolidated into her hands a necessarily large share of the power of the Egyptian priesthoods. It is important to stress in this connection that the theoretical basis of kingship in ancient Egypt was deeply rooted in religious traditions that sought to bring polarities, often couched in terms of male-female counterparts, into harmonious equilibrium. The God's Wife of Amun, as a mortal woman, made manifest the mythic ideal of the female regenerative forces that had to combine with those of the male principle in order to insure the maintenance and perpetuation of the cosmic powers responsible for creation, renewal, and resurrection. In terms of the cult of Amun, the God's Wife played a significant role. She represented his consort, often identified with the goddess Mut. Their union guaranteed the harmony of the resulting creation, because she alone could insure that her consort would be so content as to lay aside the redoubtable powers with which he might destroy as well as create. This duality of feminine wiles—the ability to titillate the god prior to effecting a successful union, and the power to assuage his anger with her amorous advances—is made manifest in the titles borne by the God's Wife. These include "the one great of [sexual] favors," "the one sweet of love," and "the one great of love" as well as "the one possessed of a comely face," "the one whose beauty calms the god," "the one enchanting of voice when she sings," and "the one who fills the room with her floral scent." Such epithets, while they might have reflected the physical beauty of any given God's Wife, are not to be taken literally, because they translate into words the aulic, or ritual, concepts this priestess was required to embody in the successful performance of her duties.

Possessed of political acumen and administrative ability, Ahmose-Nefertari enjoyed a productive political career. She distinguished herself as regent during the minority of her son, Amenhotep I, one of the early pharaohs of the eighteenth dynasty. She also survived Amenhotep I, who died childless. Perhaps as an indication of her acknowledged political standing as the dynasty's dowager queen and her continuing religious influence over the priesthoods of Amun in her capacity as God's Wife, Ahmose-Nefertari appears on monuments together with the next pharaoh, Tuthmosis I.

For several reasons, Ahmose-Nefertari continued to exercise important influence on the religious communities at Thebes even after her death. First, the position of God's Wife became hereditary and was passed on to other women who were themselves either queens or princesses. Her heirs, therefore, kept the memory of Ahmose-Nefertari alive. Second, her estate in Western Thebes continued to increase in value over time, so that each successive God's Wife was wealthier than her predecessor. Third, by virtue of her association with her son, the pharaoh Amenhotep I, who commis-

sioned a tomb for his mother in Western Thebes in which he himself subsequently was interred, Ahmose-Nefertari became a divinity (as indeed her son had). The reason for their deification is that their common tomb may have been the first to have been dug into what was to become the Valley of the Kings. To construct this tomb, Amenhotep I formed a work force in which all subsequent artisans and workers on projects in that royal necropolis were enrolled. In time, these men, dependent on the pharaohs for their livelihood, came to associate Amenhotep I with their favored lot in life and began to venerate him as an intercessor to whom one could address prayers for help or in thanksgiving. Because of her close association with him, Ahmose-Nefertari was often depicted posthumously in tomb representations sharing this role of intercessor in the company of the gods (fig. 19). She was so popular in this respect that she appears alone in such scenes no less than fifty times. Posthumous commemorative statuettes of her, sculpted of wood covered with bitumen, were also commissioned. All of these depictions forge the links binding Ahmose-Nefertari to Thebes and that city's deities.

These associations are of fundamental importance to an understanding of the family and career of Nefertari, wife of Rameses II. Before looking at her career in detail, a review of the so-called Amarna Period of the eighteenth dynasty is in order.

The Amarna Period is popularly regarded as that singular episode in ancient Egyptian history when one individual, the pharaoh Akhenaten,

FIGURE 19
The deified Ahmose-
Nefertari and her son,
Amenhotep I, are depicted
in a kiosk in this painted
vignette from the Tomb of
Nebamun and Ipuki. New
York, The Metropolitan
Museum of Art, Rogers
Fund, 1930, inv. 30.4.158.

attempted a religious revolution by which the worship of the *aton*, or sun disk, was promoted at the expense of all other religious expressions. Although a great deal has been written about this period, a great deal more investigation is required before a consensus can be reached regarding the exact nature of this religious reform.

Akhenaten was a son of Queen Tiye and Amenhotep III, the latter himself a son and immediate successor of the pharaoh Tuthmosis IV and Mutemwiya. Queen Tiye is known to have been a daughter of one Yuya and his wife, Tuya. The traditionally held opinion that her marriage was motivated by Amenhotep III's love for a commoner may require dismissal in light of the fact that it occurred when the pharaoh was so young as to suggest that it had to have been arranged. Moreover, the Egyptian names Tuya and Tiye not only are variations of the same pet name or nickname but may be synonymous abbreviations for the name Nefertari. Accordingly, both the maternal grandmother, Tuya, and the mother, Tiye, of Akhenaten bore a variation of the name of Ahmose-Nefertari, the woman associated with the political and religious traditions of the state god Amun at Thebes at the beginning of the eighteenth dynasty. This observation accords well with another one, namely that the cult of Ahmose-Nefertari flourished in Western Thebes during the reign of Amenhotep III, suggesting that Queen Tiye, with the approval and support of her husband, encouraged the commemoration of her illustrious ancestor. Indeed, the influence of Queen Tiye—not only in the court of her husband but also, after his death, in the affairs of their son Akhenaten— appears to have been patterned on the activities of Ahmose-Nefertari during the reigns of her husband, Ahmose, and son, Amenhotep I.

**FIGURE 20**

This detail of the right-hand side of a painted limestone shrine façade shows (from left to right) Akhenaten, Nefertiti, and one of their daughters beneath the rays of the *aton*. Cairo, Egyptian Museum inv. JE 65041.

If one accepts that a familial relationship existed between Queen Tiye, the wife of Amenhotep III, and Ahmose-Nefertari, the wife of Ahmose and mother of Amenhotep I, the prominent re-emergence of this collateral, female branch of the royal family of the Egyptian New Kingdom neatly explains several otherwise perplexing questions about Akhenaten, his successors, and their wives.

Although the pharaoh Akhenaten was followed by several individuals whose identity is often contested, the order of succession from Tutankhamun to Ay to Horemhab to Rameses I is fixed. This unbroken line of succession is significant on two counts. First, it has been suggested that the Egyptian names Yuya and Ay are, on the model provided for the names Tuya/Tiye, variations of a pet name or nickname and synonymous abbreviations for a putative longer name, the exact form of which is debated. In this case, Queen Tiye's father, Yuya, and the pharaoh Ay would be like-named, suggesting a familial relationship as well, a relationship supported by their shared military titles, assumed to have been inherited. These men would therefore appear to have been members of the same family. The pharaoh Ay thus becomes a relative of Akhenaten, from whose maternal grandfather he appears to have been descended.

Horemhab, the last pharaoh of the eighteenth dynasty, was not related by birth in any way to any member of these royal families. He ascended the throne as pharaoh by virtue of his unchallenged position as commander-in-chief of the army and as Ay's undisputed deputy. (Succession did not necessarily run through family lines.) He married Mutnodjmet, who is suggested to have been one of the many important daughters of Ay, his immediate predecessor. In fact, some have gone so far as to suggest that Akhenaten's wife Nefertiti (fig. 20) may have been another of Ay's daughters.

Nefertari, the wife of Rameses II and the subject of our study, also appears to have been a daughter of Ay. She therefore could have been related on her father's side to both Queen Nefertiti and Queen Mutnodjmet. The evidence for this, while slight, is compelling. It comes in the form of a faience knob, originally from a wooden box, around which a string could be wrapped and secured by sealing it with stamped wax or clay, thereby insuring the safety of its contents (fig. 21). Discovered in the Tomb of Nefertari by Schiaparelli, this knob, now in the Museo Egizio, is inscribed with the throne name of the pharaoh Ay. Egyptologists have suggested that objects found in royal tombs bearing a royal name other than that of the tomb's owner are generally family heirlooms belonging to a relative. Invoking this suggestion for this faience knob would make Nefertari a daughter—the only relationship chronologically possible— of the pharaoh Ay and a younger sister of both Queen Nefertiti and Queen Mutnodjmet.

There appears to be a second, if somewhat veiled, reference to the Amarna Period in the corridor inscriptions in the Tomb of Nefertari that accompany the goddess Isis. They contain a spell alluding to the sun god, Re. The word used in this context is *itn*, meaning the *aton*, or sun disk, that

The faience knob inscribed with the name of the pharaoh Ay that was discovered in the Tomb of Nefertari by Schiaparelli. Turin, Museo Egizio inv. S. 5162.

This heiress theory, alternately termed the right of matrilinear succession, cannot be maintained, because the majority of pharaohs in the course of the eighteenth and nineteenth dynasties were either proclaimed by their fathers as their successors or elevated to the throne by adoption.

On the contrary, the association of these pharaohs with the women of this collateral branch of the royal family was linked to the fundamental role the latter played in the cult of the state god Amun, a position of status and authority established by the revered Ahmose-Nefertari at the beginning of the eighteenth dynasty. Their association with the pharaohs reinforced the theological basis of Egyptian kingship whereby secular peace and tranquility throughout the realm were linked to the ability of the goddess, in the guise of a priestess, to allay the destructive forces of the god and insure the god and goddess' sanctified union for the continuing harmony and stability of the universe. In these terms, it is completely understandable that a pharaoh such as Amenhotep III, whose reign represents the apogee of Egyptian culture during the eighteenth dynasty, would have aligned himself by marriage with a daughter of a family ostensibly related to Ahmose-Nefertari, because his reign was inextricably linked to Thebes and associated with Amun, that city's supreme deity. Egypt was, after all, the undisputed mistress of the known eastern Mediterranean basin, Thebes was her unrivaled capital, and the prestige of Theban Amun and his priesthoods was without rival in Egypt. The pharaohs' association with the fam-

figured so prominently in the religious reform of Akhenaten. *Itn* is used rather than *re*, which the context seems to demand. This particular spell, which Isis recites for the benefit of Nefertari, translates, "I give to thee a place within the sacred land in the presence of the god Wennefer [a form of Osiris]. Mayest thou appear like the *aton* forever!"

If one subscribes to this attractive suggestion that Nefertari is, indeed, to be connected with the personalities and events of the Amarna Period, one adduces a remarkable family tree in which a putative collateral branch of the Amarna family produced one pharaoh in King Ay and four queens in the persons of Tiye, the wife of Amenhotep III, and each of Ay's three daughters: Nefertiti, wife of Akhenaten; Mutnodjmet, wife of Horemheb; and Nefertari, principal wife of Rameses II. The reason for the prominence of these women has little to do with the now outdated suggestion that a new pharaoh's claim to the throne depended on his relationship to a principal female of his predecessor's family.

ily of Ahmose-Nefertari was indicative of the peace enjoyed by the court and the harmony exercised by the priesthoods.

The female members of this family fell into disfavor with Akhenaten because his reforms were antagonistic to the very priesthood from which they derived their status. Gradually, the role played by Queen Nefertiti diminished; her power and influence waned toward the end of her husband's reign. Not only had Akhenaten distanced himself from her family by gradually diminishing her importance; he had also intentionally ruptured the role of the family's women as the mortal manifestation of the mythic female principle in the cosmic order by depriving the *aton* of a mythological consort. There was no female counterpart of the *aton* in the religion created by Akhenaten.

Alienating the family, tampering with the underlying theological tenets of Egyptian religion by discarding the female principle, proscribing the cult of Amun, and—further—relocating Egypt's capital from Thebes to the site generally known as Amarna undermined the influence, wealth, and importance of the members of this collateral branch, whose women could claim with justification that their ancestors had safeguarded the deities of Egypt and their temples at precisely the time when their menfolk delivered Egypt from the hands of her foes during the wars of liberation at the dynasty's beginning.

The deaths of the pharaoh Akhenaten and his immediate successor(s) effectively reversed the trends established during his reign. This reversal was no doubt encouraged by members of the royal family who were now free to re-establish their former positions of prestige and power. Tutankhamun, who had been known as Tutankhaton, changed his name, and the capital was transferred back to Thebes from Amarna. These were but two of the more obvious signs that Egypt had returned to orthodoxy. The elevation to the throne, following Tutankhamun's death, of the aged Ay, himself perhaps a scion of the venerable family of Ahmose-Nefertari, can be regarded as a conscious attempt to restore the status quo of the Amun priesthoods in their collective efforts to regain the prestige and wealth destroyed by the iconoclasm of Akhenaten's pogrom. Ay's ascension thereby insured this priesthood of its former position, a position that was further consolidated by the marriage of his daughter, Mutnodjmet, to Horemheb, his successor. Mutnodjmet, whose very name, "Sweet Is the Goddess Mut [consort of the god Amun]," is associated with Thebes and its deities, recalls the epithets of the God's Wife, and seems to imply a conscious choice indicative of the renewed popularity of the Theban deities and of the support enjoyed by their priesthoods. Horemheb not only restored the monuments to Amun at Karnak and granted his wife the status enjoyed by her ancestors but also ordered the aggressive destruction of the *aton* temple in East Karnak by directing his agents to put it to the torch.

**FIGURE 22**

This image of Nefertari, standing with her arm raised, is found beside the left leg of the southernmost colossal statue of her husband in the eastern colonnade of the Court of Rameses II, Temple of Luxor.

## Nefertari as Chief Queen and Principal Wife

The cultic importance of Thebes and the determining role played by the queen are fundamental to an understanding of the early career of Nefertari, which in its own way reflects the central importance of this city and the haunting memory of the Amarna interlude in the midst of the realities of a changing world. It is therefore to those changes that we must turn, and to the Hittites, who brought them about.

The Hittites, peoples who occupied the heartland of

central Anatolia (in modern Turkey), appear in ancient Egyptian records with increasing frequency from the reign of Amenhotep III on. One of their kings, Suppiluliumas, engaged in diplomatic correspondence in an effort to establish an alliance with Akhenaten and, after the death of this pharaoh, even received a request from an as yet unidentified Egyptian queen or princess for the hand of one of his sons in marriage. Initially suspecting a ruse, but eventually acceding to the request, Suppiluliumas dispatched one of his sons, Zannanza by name, to Egypt, but the hapless youth was murdered en route under circumstances about which the Egyptian sources are silent. Suppiluliumas's campaign to avenge the death of Zannanza was interrupted by a plague outbreak. Horemhab, who had become pharaoh and who was himself a career military officer, recognized the potential threat of the Hittites. Being childless, he took steps to insure Egypt's security by selecting as his successor the military commander Paramese, whose career in many ways paralleled that of Horemhab himself and who was also not of royal lineage.

On the death of Horemhab, Paramese, a man of advanced years, ascended the throne as Rameses I, thereby inaugurating the nineteenth dynasty. The geopolitical axis of Egypt had by this time shifted from Thebes to the eastern delta, the homeland of this new pharaoh's military family and the region from which his descendants were to rule. This was doubtless due to its geographic proximity to the theater of military campaigns directed against the Hittites, which were to escalate over time. It appears that

Rameses I succeeded in reasserting Egypt's claim to territories in Nubia, the Sinai, and the area of modern Syria-Palestine, to judge from monuments found there that bear his name.

Rameses I was married to Satre. Although their family is assumed to have been large, only Sety, Rameses I's successor, is known by name. Sety appears to have been one of the couple's oldest children, an assumption reinforced by the observation that he was already an adult when his father possibly designated him as co-regent and heir apparent. While serving in his father's court, Sety was already married to Tuy, who was his only wife. She was not of royal birth and was not related in any way to the women of the collateral branch of the royal family. (The seeming similarity between her name and theirs is merely due to the way Egyptian hieroglyphs are transliterated into English.) During this time, the son of Sety and Tuy, the future Rameses II (husband of Nefertari), was born.

A capable ruler, excellent field commander, and energetic builder, Sety I embarked on a series of military campaigns in the first year of his reign in an effort to re-establish Egypt's empire. By his sixth regnal year, he had successfully reclaimed all territory formerly under Egyptian control up to the city of Kadesh, which reverted to the Hittites. Sety I was able to reach a peaceful accord with Muwatali, the Hittite king, by which each sovereign recognized the other's territorial claims and agreed to a cessation of hostilities. It was during this time that the future pharaoh Rameses II, though a mere boy of about ten, was given the honorific title of commander-in-chief of the army. Although the youth did not campaign, the conferring of this title was a clear indication that Sety I regarded him, even at this time, as his heir and successor. This position was clarified further a few years later, when Sety I publicly acclaimed and formally invested Rameses as the heir apparent with the official title of prince regent.

With the political situation abroad in hand and with the prospect of a peaceful transference of power to his son, Sety I, following the precedent established by his father, turned his attention to religious matters. Although he favored the eastern delta cities close to his ancestral home and did much to promote the cult of the god Ptah at Memphis, Sety I went to great lengths to appease the priesthoods at Thebes. This homage to Amun was part of a conscious program, the aim of which was the eradication of the memory of the pharaohs of the Amarna Period, an episode that continued to cast its haunting shadow across the religious landscape of the land. So intent was Sety I in his efforts to proscribe the memory of Akhenaten and the other pharaohs of the Amarna Period that he ordered the excision of their names from the official lists of Egyptian pharaohs. The conscious condemnation of the memory of this episode of their history by Sety I and others may explain why the ancient Egyptian evidence that has survived for the Amarna interlude is both so scarce and so fragmented.

Sety I did not neglect the collateral branch of the royal family whose female members had done so much to promote the cult of Amun. It was doubtless because of his need to demonstrate support for both the Theban priesthood and the members of that collateral branch that he arranged for his son, the prince regent Rameses, to marry Nefertari. As husband and wife, the couple lived at Sety's court. Before the coronation of her husband Rameses II as pharaoh, Nefertari was the mother of at least one child, their firstborn, Prince Amenkherkhepeshef.

If Nefertari was in fact a daughter of the collateral branch of the eighteenth-dynasty royal family, Sety's choice of daughter-in-law effectively drew the Theban priesthood back into the ruling family's circle. So closely aligned to Thebes was Nefertari herself that she incorporated the phrase Meryenmut, "the one beloved of the goddess Mut [consort of the Theban god Amun]," into her name when she married. The overtures of Sety I to this Theban family extended even to his wife, Tuy, who received the title of God's Wife of Amun. Sety also dedicated a double temple in Western Thebes to the memories of Queen Tiye, wife of Amenhotep III, and the revered Ahmose-Nefertari.

Almost nothing is known of Nefertari's appearance. Her name, which may be translated as either "The Most Beautiful of Them" or "The Very Best," does not apparently belie her beauty; her husband said of his bride that she was "comparable with the beauties of the palace." Indeed, an anonymous tourist visiting the Temple of Luxor in antiquity was apparently so enthralled with the image of Nefertari standing beside the leg of one of her husband's statues (fig. 22) that he scratched a graffito of an archer

FIGURE 23

The graffito of an archer
on the column adjacent to
a colossal statue of
Rameses II (see fig. 22).

which he dutifully identified by an
accompanying inscription as Paris (fig.
23). No doubt he did this because Nefertari's figure reminded him of the legend-
ary beauty of Helen of Troy, whom the
goddess Aphrodite granted to the Trojan
Paris, a mortal, when Paris declared
Aphrodite the fairest of deities. Called
"God's Wife" at least once, Nefertari
bore as a consequence a string of aulic
epithets describing her as "one possessed
of charm, sweetness, and love, who
occupies a [special] place within the
Temple of Amun."

Arranged though this marriage may
have been, Nefertari from the moment of
her wedding became the king's unrivaled
partner and cocelebrant, positions of
status and privilege she enjoyed until her
death about twenty years after his
coronation. The fact that she could
maintain such an iron-fisted grasp on her
status is a remarkable tribute to her
inner strength and intelligence, particularly when one realizes that Rameses II
had a large harem that included at least
four other notable Egyptian women and

a Hittite princess, known by her Egyptian
name of Maathorneferure, whom he
married after Nefertari's death. The
pattern for Nefertari's appearance on
monuments throughout her career was
established in the very first year of her
husband's reign as king, when, for
example, she was associated with him at
a monument in Silsila West.

Of the more than approximately two
hundred children fathered by Rameses
II, his firstborn son, Amenkherkhepeshef, was Nefertari's child, as were his
third, eleventh, and sixteenth sons and
fourth and fifth daughters.

Although religious practice and tradition generally excluded representations
of living queens from the relief decoration
of temples during the New Kingdom—
particularly during the eighteenth
dynasty—Nefertari is depicted in the
Luxor temple (fig. 24). Here she is shown
wearing a tightly fitting sheath and
tripartite wig beneath a vulture headdress. From the time of the Old Kingdom,
the feather headdress was the emblem of
the titular goddesses of Upper and
Lower Egypt, Nekhbet and Wadjet, and
was soon associated with queens as
well as with the goddesses Isis and Mut.
This headdress also became associated
with the God's Wife of Amun in the
eighteenth dynasty. Here it supports
double plumes—first attested as queenly
regalia in the thirteenth dynasty—
which allude to several deities, among
whom are Amun and Min, god of fertility. (Nefertari speaks of herself as Min in
one instance in her tomb: "I am Min in
his setting out, as he put the two feathers
on my head." On one of her statues now
in Cairo, Nefertari is described as "the

one comely of face who is also beautiful
with respect to the two feathers.") In her
lowered hand she grasps a *menat*, a
ceremonial implement made of several
strings of beads connected to a counter-
poise, while in her raised hand she
holds a sistrum, or sacred rattle, which is
the subject of the inscription between
her hands, *Shaking the two sistra for her
father[, Amun]*. Such musical perfor-
mances were associated with the rituals
performed by the God's Wife in Thebes.

Memories of Akhenaten, revived
perhaps by Rameses II's marriage to
Nefertari, may have helped him to forge
a causal link, however tenuous, by which
he connected the loss of Egypt's empire
with the policies of the earlier pharaoh.
Seemingly obsessed with this link,
Rameses II renewed hostilities against
the Hittite king Muwatali, with whom
Sety I had earlier achieved rapproche-
ment. Marshaling his troops, Rameses II
departed for Syria, intent on breaking
the influence of the Hittites in the region
by capturing Kadesh, their stronghold.
The battle was apparently a draw.
Repeatedly over the course of the next
decade, Rameses II marched into battle
in this same theater of operations,
though many of his victories were often
reversed shortly after his return to Egypt.
This back-and-forth continued into the
reign of the Hittite king Hattusili III,
who had gained the throne by a palace
coup which drove his nephew, Urhi-
Teshub, into exile. Urhi-Teshub eventually arrived at the delta residence of
Rameses II, where the two formed an
alliance aimed at deposing Hattusili III
and his chief queen, Pudukhepa. As
Hattusili marched against Egypt, the

Hittites were simultaneously attacked by
Assyria. Thus Hattusili III was forced
to sue for peace with Rameses II. The
resulting treaty, signed by both rulers, is
history's first mutual nonaggression
pact. Copies are preserved both in
Egyptian hieroglyphs and in cuneiform,
the wedge-shaped writing employed at

FIGURE 24
Nefertari, shaking
a sistrum, or sacred rattle,
is preceded by her
husband, Rameses II, who
makes an offering to
Amun. This relief is on the
inner face of the First Pylon
at the Temple of Luxor.

this time in the ancient Near East as the language for diplomatic correspondence.

As a result of the treaty, Hattusili III and Pudukhepa initiated a series of letters, the former writing to Rameses II and the latter to Nefertari. One of Nefertari's replies survives on a clay tablet on which her name is rendered into cuneiform as Naptera; she refers to Pudukhepa as her sister. This letter may be paraphrased as follows:

Naptera, the Great Queen of Egypt, says, "Deliver this message to Pudukhepa, the Great Queen of the Hatti [Hittites], my sister, so that she may hear my words, namely, with me, your sister, all goes well; with my country all goes well. With you, my sister, may all go well; with your country may all go well! Realize that I have duly noted that you, my sister, have corresponded with me inquiring both about my well-being and about the relationships of good peace and brotherhood into which the Great King, the King of Egypt, has entered with his brother, the Great King, the King of Hatti.

May the Egyptian sun god and the Hittite storm god bring you joy; and may the sun god cause the achieved peace to be good and may he bestow good brotherhood on the Great King, the King of Egypt, and on his brother, the Great King, the King of the Hatti, forever. And I am in friendship and sororial relationships with my sister, the Great Queen of the Hatti, now and forever!"

However stilted and repetitive its phrasing may seem, this document is nevertheless very intimate. Its contents enable us to see how Nefertari, separated by language and distance and operating

in a vacuum (the etiquette of diplomatic correspondence between royal women had not been established), nevertheless attempted to bridge these chasms with a personal letter. Her telling words were accompanied by the exchange of gifts; those sent to Pudukhepa included jewelry, dyed textiles, and royal garments. Few ancient queens have left posterity such windows on their worlds.

With the Hittites now firmly allied with the Egyptians, Rameses II could again cast his eyes to the far southern reaches of his realm. At Abu Simbel (fig. 25), below the Tropic of Cancer, he brought to conclusion the construction and decoration of two temples, the northern one of which is associated with the goddess Hathor and Nefertari herself. (Both of these temples were threatened in this century by the waters rising behind the Aswan High Dam and, in an effort to preserve them, were moved to higher ground between January 1966 and September 1968 by an international campaign conducted under the auspices of UNESCO.) Rameses II's motivation for the construction of these colossal rock-cut sanctuaries has been the subject of much debate, but one thing is certain. He singled out Nefertari for special treatment here; she was the only one of his queens so honored. In fact, he clarified her role both in his reign and at this site by means of an inscription that reads, in part, *[Rameses II] made the [northern] temple [at Abu Simbel], a very great monument, for the principal chief queen, Nefertarimeryenmut, for whose very sake the sun does shine!* The reference, despite a modern reader's penchant to see a sentimental allusion to a hus-

band's love for his wife, is clearly cultic. The southern, or main, temple of Rameses II at Abu Simbel was constructed in such a way that twice a year, in February and October, the rays of the rising sun would penetrate the axis of the temple at dawn and illuminate the four statues of the gods—one of which represents Rameses II himself—cut from the living rock in the rearmost wall of the sanctuary. Rameses II unequivocally linked himself and his cult to that of the sun god Re and, by extension, to that of Amun at Abu Simbel. As a result, Nefertari, in her various capacities as priestess and God's Wife and by virtue of her association with Hathor, continued to provide the theological basis for her husband's reign. As a manifestation of the female principle, her ministrations

at Abu Simbel insured the sunrise, thereby guaranteeing the harmonious cyclic recreation of the cosmos with the forces of chaos held in check. It is to this cultic capacity that the passage just quoted refers. And it is precisely to this association with the cult of the Egyptian sun god that Nefertari refers in her letter to Pudukhepa.

Elsewhere at Abu Simbel one finds conflicting statements about the person responsible for the construction of the northern temple. In several passages, Rameses II claims responsibility: "He, Rameses II, made it as his monument for the principal wife of the king, Nefertari-meryenmut, a house hewn in the pure mountain of Nubia of fine, white and enduring sandstone, as an eternal work." But elsewhere one finds this passage:

FIGURE 25

The façade of the Temple of Hathor at Abu Simbel includes images of Nefertari alternating with those of her husband.

"The principal wife of the king, Nefertarimeryenmut; she is the one who made
a house [i.e., this temple] in the pure
mountain." The last passage would seem
to indicate that Nefertari had a hand in
the planning of the temple. Such an
activity is entirely consistent with the
significant role she played in the reign of
her husband and throughout her lifetime.
The monumental proportions of her two
colossal statues, arranged between
those of her husband, would tend to
support this contention, as would the
observation that Rameses II himself was
worshiped as a deity within the southern
temple. If Nefertari was involved in the
construction at this site, and if the cult of
her divine husband as performed there
was dependent on the successful dis-
charge of her sacred and divine functions,
there is every reason to expect that she
would have insisted on the same cultic,
divine privileges for herself.

The northern temple at Abu Simbel is,
however, a bittersweet monument to
Nefertari. Whereas its cultic program
may indeed proclaim her divinity and
declare her paramount importance
within the reign of her husband, the
events surrounding the dedication of the
temples at Abu Simbel imply both her
eclipse and death. In Rameses II's twenty-
fourth regnal year, he traveled south to
celebrate the inauguration of these
stupendous temples. On a rock-cut
commemorative stela sculpted into one
of the mountains at Abu Simbel, we find
him accompanied not by Nefertari, but
by the princess Meritamun. The queen is
merely represented below this scene in
another one, in which she is depicted as
an enthroned recipient of offerings. Her

FIGURE 26
This statue of Rameses II is
considered to be one of
the finest sculpted during
his reign. Turin, Museo
Egizio inv. 1380.

54

absence from the principal scene is re-markable. Was she ill? Had she died? Or had she, near the end of her career, been replaced by another? We can only spec-ulate. One thing is certain. At about the time of the opening ceremonies at Abu Simbel, Nefertari disappears from the archaeological record. There is no evi-dence to suggest the cause of her death.

So important a queen and so dominant a personality was Nefertari that her monuments could not be summarily destroyed nor her name readily hacked out or replaced by that of another. As a result, at Thebes and at Abu Simbel, as elsewhere, her monuments continue to proclaim her presence to this day. How-ever, certain other monuments seem to have been altered at some point after her death in order to demonstrate that her memory would have no value in the dynastic succession. These include a masterfully sculpted statue of Rameses II seated (fig. 26) and another statue, also of him, found at Karnak. When one looks carefully at a detail of the former depicting a queen (fig. 27), one sees that both the name accompanying this figure and its upraised arm were intentionally destroyed. The statue found at Karnak is similarly damaged. This conscious effacing may have been an attempt by agents of Merneptah, a son and successor of Rameses II, to remove the image and name of Nefertari from these statues.

Rameses himself ruled until he was well over ninety years old. Many of his more than a hundred sons assuredly predeceased him; in their number were certainly those born early in his reign to Nefertari. With her death some forty years before his, and with the supposed deaths of her sons in the interim, another queen, Isetnofret, and her sons must have come to the fore. One of the latter, Merneptah by name, ultimately emerged as his father's heir and successor. Already in his late sixties when he became pharaoh, Merneptah may have been responsible for effacing the names and image of Nefertari from these two monuments of his father in an effort to minimize her importance and distance himself from her family.

FIGURE 27

Detail of figure 26 showing intentional damage to the image and title of Nefertari.

**FIGURE 28**

This unfinished painting in the
Tomb of Nakht retains traces of
the grid that enabled the
artists to establish appropriate
proportional relationships
among the various elements in
the scene. New York, The
Metropolitan Museum of Art,
Rogers Fund, 1915, inv. 15.5.19f.

# On the Nature of
Egyptian Painting

he advent of the nineteenth dynasty ushered in a change by which only the mothers of pharaohs, their queens, and their children were permitted to be interred within the Valley of the Queens (fig. 2). These burials were grouped by reign into clearly defined plots of real estate. Rameses II, on becoming pharaoh, designated a sector in the northern part of the valley as the area reserved for his family. To date, the tombs of his mother, Tuy, of several of his daughters, and

of Nefertari have been identified. Continued archaeological exploration may reveal the tombs of his other wives Isisnofret and Henetmire, which are mentioned in contemporary documents as being located in the Valley of the Queens.

Whereas most of the tombs in the Valley of the Queens conform to a simple plan in which a series of successive chambers is cut into the limestone in a straight line, the plan of the Tomb of Nefertari is more elaborate (fig. 3). In fact, its plan and decoration—primarily large-scale depictions of the queen before deities rather than vignettes and texts from various religious books of the underworld—are closer to those of the tombs of the pharaohs of the eighteenth dynasty in the Valley of the Kings than to either the other tombs in the Valley of the Queens or the royal tombs of the nineteenth dynasty in the Valley of the Kings. The Joint EAO-GCI Nefertari Conservation Project has stabilized the paintings in the tomb to a point where one can profitably discuss their place in the history of ancient Egyptian art and also catch a fleeting glimpse of the special group of men from whose ranks came the artisans who decorated it.

Although the issue is debatable, the evidence appears to suggest the existence in ancient Egypt, in some form or other, of pattern books to which the decorators of tombs and their patrons had recourse for the selection of motifs and texts. Once selected, these scenes and texts were transferred to the wall by means of a series of grids which not only established the proportional relationships between the elements in any given scene

but also accommodated a combination of scenes in such a way that all of the available space was comfortably filled.

One individual, termed the "outline scribe," played a major role in the processes just described. This role can be appreciated by examining a so-called unfinished scene from the tomb of the official Nakht (Number 52) at Thebes (fig. 28). Remains of the grid lines, painted in red, are visible running through the hair of the seated figures at top left as well as through the legs of their chair. The images were designed by the outline scribe within the grid with a very strong contour line, which can be compared to those found in coloring books from which young children are taught to draw. The comparison is not an idle one, because the strong contour lines in ancient Egyptian art, like those in children's coloring books, were intended to keep the applied colors trapped within them. One can judge how this process was effected in ancient Egypt by turning to this same unfinished scene. The color patches can be profitably compared to those passages of the scene which were defined by the contours but left unpainted.

The limitation imposed by the contour line was further reinforced by the fact that the artisan charged with "coloring in" the contours was restricted by the color terminology of the ancient Egyptian language, which generally admitted only five color words: *kem* (black), *khedj* (white), *desher* (red), *wadj* (blue or green), and *sab* (variegated). Attempting to reconcile this ancient terminology with terms used for the colors of light refracted through a prism, one immediately sees that the spectrum of red/ orange/yellow was reduced to the one word *desher*, whereas the spectrum of green/blue/indigo/violet was embodied in the word *wadj*. The reflection and absorption of all colors were termed *khedj* and *kem*, respectively. Objects that seemingly appeared mottled to the eyes of the ancient Egyptians were termed *sab* without any attempt to define the relationships between colors perceived. As a result, the ancient Egyptian painter thought in terms of a limited palette, the colors of which had to be applied in solid patches restricted by contour lines from spilling over into adjacent areas.

These stringent rules were the same as those jewelers observed in the manufacture of objects (fig. 29). This comparison, demonstrating the uniformity of the approach followed by artisans in different crafts, is significant for several reasons. Color confined to specific areas could be, and was, imbued with symbolic meaning. However, the fact that their color vocabulary was so limited impelled the ancient Egyptians to adopt a pluralistic view with regard to that symbolism. As a result, reds and greens/blues might connote resurrection and regeneration, respectively, whereas the same reds in other contexts might equally suggest overtones of chaos and evil.

In the vignettes in the sarcophagus chamber in the Tomb of Nefertari (figs. 16, 17), the exclusive use of yellowish ocher hues for the figures and their accompanying hieroglyphic inscriptions, which are painted over a white background and articulated by details picked out in reds and blacks, is a conscious

effort to imitate the color of gold, a precious metal that neither rusts nor tarnishes. As a result of these properties, the ancient Egyptians associated gold and its color with the concepts of permanence and indestructibility, characteristics suitable for the flesh of their eternal deities. Because of these associations, gold—either in the form of metal or as paint—imparted to the objects it adorned

**FIGURE 29**

The gold on this vulture headdress was formed into individual cells which then were filled with pieces of other materials. These pieces created solid patches of color, producing the same effect achieved by painters. The Cleveland Museum of Art, John Huntington Art and Polytechnic Trust, inv. 20.1991.

**FIGURE 30**

This scene from Chamber G in the Tomb of Nefertari illustrates the method employed by ancient Egyptian painters to achieve a dappled effect in their representations of cattle.

the idea of incorruptibility. It is entirely understandable that the sarcophagus chamber of the Tomb of Nefertari should be clad in gold, since this would symbolically have insured the queen's preservation for eternity. There is no reason, therefore, to suppose, as some scholars have suggested, that the sections of this tomb decorated in this so-called monochromatic style were painted at a later date.

Ancient Egyptian painters avoided,

insofar as it was possible, both painterly effects and the use of broken color— that is, the overlapping of several hues within the same patch bounded by one contour. For example, the dappled appearance of the hides of individual animals was represented during the eighteenth dynasty by the application of each color adjacent to, as opposed to over, the color nearest to it (fig. 30). This technique was used in tomb paintings at Thebes to produce other effects as well. In some cases, the juxtaposition of hues eventually denied the contour line its power to separate them.

From the time of the Old Kingdom, the ancient Egyptians had employed variation of hue as a visual means of isolating one human figure from another in compositions in which figures were rendered with a great deal of overlapping. The artists of the eighteenth dynasty further developed the approach for their depictions of crowd scenes. When called upon to represent a group of individuals standing shoulder to shoulder, Egyptian artisans treated the composition like a deck of playing cards fanned out, so that the same outline, repeated to define each successive figure, was then colored alternately lighter or darker. One of the best-preserved examples of this

technique is found among the bearers in the Tomb of Ramose (fig. 31).

Whether these conscious juxtapositions of similar hues led to further experimentation is moot. But in many of the paintings in the tombs from the eighteenth dynasty, one sees a concomitant experiment by which a similar juxtaposition of hues was employed to render the body visible beneath transparent drapery. An early example, from the time of the pharaoh Amenhotep II, is the depiction from the Tomb of Sennefer (Number 96), in which the latter is shown standing, accompanied by his wife (fig. 32). His legs, torso, and upper arms are covered with the transparent linen fabric from which his costume was woven. These anatomical parts appear as pink color patches that contrast with

**FIGURE 31**

As can be seen in this file of bearers from the Tomb of Ramose, Egyptian artists differentiated individuals standing shoulder to shoulder by fanning the forms out and defining each figure by the application of alternately lighter and darker colors.

**FIGURE 32**
In this scene from the Tomb of Sennefer, the artists employed a lighter color for his legs, arms, and torso to indicate the transparent nature of his clothing.

the red tones of his feet and ankles, lower arms, and face. From these and other like examples, it would appear that the artisans of this period actively exploited the potential inherent in a tradition that allowed for the application of modulated values of one and the same hue in adjacent color patches.

The culmination of this technique for rendering the transparency of finely woven linen and the body underneath can be observed in two registers from the Tomb of Nebamun and Ipuki (Number 181), dated to the time of Amenhotep III, where one sees men and women preparing themselves for a banquet (fig. 33). Skin tones are rendered here in two distinct manners. The first relies on

**FIGURE 34**

The forms of Nefertari's
body emerging from
beneath her gossamer
costume are clearly evident
in this representation from
Chamber G of her tomb.

the technique just described, in which fanned-out faces are depicted as alternating patches of juxtaposed lighter and darker values of the same hue. The second is a somewhat more sophisticated attempt to convey by the application of paint the suggestion that the bodies of some of the men and women are emerging from beneath their draperies. The upper torsos of the women and the upper torsos and thighs of the men are painted a honey color that is feathered out into the white area representing the textile, the folds of which are rendered as stripes of ocher applied directly on top of it.

This one scene therefore contains two of the exceptions to the general rule that ancient Egyptian painters confined color by means of contours. The paucity of documents and absence of an ample color terminology thwart attempts to define, in precise terms, the objectives of such approaches. It has, however, been suggested that such passages were created by artisans interacting freely and directly with their medium. Once developed, these techniques became part of the repertoire of decorative effects to which any subsequent painter might have had recourse.

So the rendering of the body emerging from beneath transparent drapery became an easily applied formula; examples can be found in any number of tomb paintings from the nineteenth and twentieth dynasties. Albeit in a somewhat restrained form, it was applied as well to certain representations of Queen Nefertari in her tomb in the Valley of the Queens (fig. 34). The fullness of the gossamer garments she wears, doubtless due to the fact that they were composed

FIGURE 35
Chamber C, south wall:
Nefertari playing senet.

of several yards of material, afforded her a greater degree of mobility than that permitted by the traditional sheath. This difference has been interpreted as indicative of the greater personal freedom enjoyed by Egyptian women of the New Kingdom. Although garments woven of this type of linen allowed artists to depict a woman's breast and thighs, it is important to note that in her tomb Nefertari—save in the one vignette in which she is shown playing *senet* (fig. 35)—is depicted more modestly. In fact, in most of the scenes in which she is represented in the company of a goddess, it is the goddess who is depicted topless.

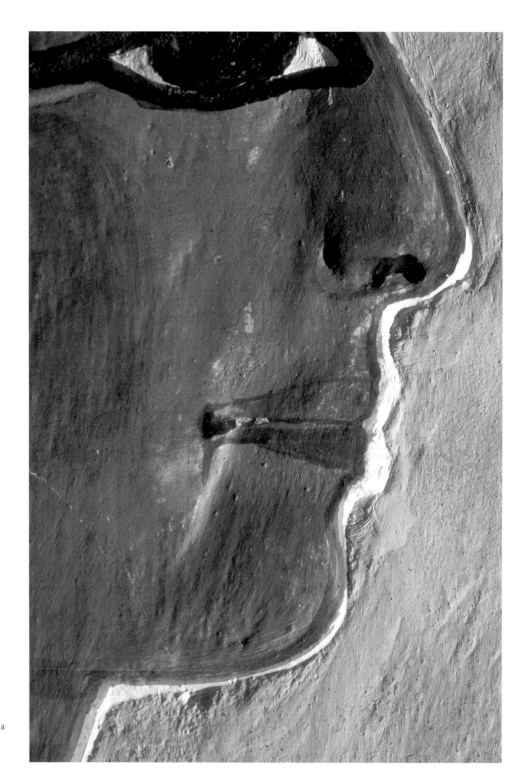

FIGURE 36
The treatment of
Nefertari's face in her
tomb sometimes reveals a
nascent chiaroscuro.

# An Assessment
# of the Wall Paintings

t is of fundamental importance for a fuller understanding of ancient Egyptian art to realize that the rendering of the illusion of the male or female body emerging from beneath a garment was achieved at least five hundred years before a similar phenomenon is detectable in the art of ancient Greece. The restraint shown by the artisans in the depiction of Nefertari's body emerging from beneath her costume at first draws our attention away from the most extraordinary characteristic of

some of the paintings in her tomb, namely the treatment of her face (fig. 36). Here, for the first time in the history of art, a painter treated the human face as a three-dimensional volume. Values of red and mauve were combined in the same color patches, integrated by the absence of contours, so that a nascent chiaroscuro, or modeling of light and dark, was achieved. Although this technique is to be found in selected vignettes from at least two other, nearly contemporary tombs, those of Userhet (fig. 37) and of Ipy, and may perhaps be traced back to as early as the eighteenth dynasty, none of the earlier examples are as accomplished. Moreover, this technique was reserved exclusively for depictions

FIGURE 37
The facial details in this scene in the Tomb of Userhet, painted during the reign of Sety I, anticipate the nascent chiaroscuro found in some renderings of Nefertari in her tomb.

of Nefertari in her tomb. The artisans responsible for this remarkable technical innovation, assuredly drawn from the ranks of the "servants in the place of truth," as the craftsmen working on the royal tombs were anciently called, were gifted individuals who recognized the great potential inherent in combining values of the same hue within a color patch devoid of contour lines. Furthermore, these craftsmen exercised a degree of artistic freedom because they did not always slavishly follow the contour lines as drawn by the outline scribes and carved in the plaster. Occasionally, one sees a double contour resulting from the painter's decision to refine the profile of a face by disregarding its original design or by modifying the shape of a wig (fig. 38).

This spirit of creativity enabled the painters to add another dimension to their innovative use of color. As we have seen, color in ancient Egyptian art was imbued with meaning. Reds were generally reserved for skin tones of men, while yellows were employed for those of women. This was because men, whose activities took place outdoors, reacted naturally to the sun and tanned, whereas women, who were—despite their apparently privileged status—expected to confine themselves to the home, remained pale. (There are, of course, exceptions to this generalization.)

According to this practice, Nefertari ought invariably to have been painted yellow, the color of women, as indeed she is on some of the pillars in her tomb. The fact that elsewhere her skin is painted with mauves and pinks, colors that can be described as *desher*, or red, is not without significance. One could argue

that she was painted in reddish hues because she was active in the world of men, in the "outdoors" of politics and world affairs. The importance of Nefertari and her family connections for the reign of Sety I has been articulated above. Those ties of prestige, authority, and power—familial, political, and religious—which she brought to her marriage to Rameses II are all emphasized by the use of reds for her flesh tones in her tomb. Her special role is further emphasized by the fact that she is the only mortal represented there. She is, therefore, the principal celebrant and interacts in each scene with the deities of Egypt as if she were the pharaoh. Nefertari is presented for eternity as the sovereign authority in Western Thebes, ascribing to herself the role of ruler and priest. It is doubtless for this reason that her costumes conceal, rather than reveal, her femininity (fig. 17).

For all of these reasons, those tomb paintings of Nefertari which are rendered with light and dark values of the same hue rank among the finest masterpieces of ancient Egyptian painting. The exceptional technique and use of reds were unequivocally intended to proclaim the message that she was an exceptional individual. In the present state of knowledge, these tomb paintings are unique. We must therefore exercise extreme caution before citing these examples in support of sweeping conclusions about the nature of Egyptian painting, which both before and after this very brief interlude conforms generally to the practice of exhibiting contour-locked patches of color.

The artisans responsible for decorating

the Tomb of Nefertari masterfully combined this innovative use of "chiaroscuro" and novel use of reds for her flesh tones with more traditional elements. Turning again to her face, we see an aquiline profile in which the nostril is prominent. The flesh of the throat is indicated by a series of parallel lines. Even without earrings, the earlobe is nevertheless shown pierced. These details of the face are exactly those established for representations dated to the reign of Sety I, as found in the relief decoration of his temple at Abydos or in those from his tomb. Ultimately, they derive from the repertoire of forms available to the artisans in the employ of Amenhotep III. Accordingly, one can observe how the artisans working in the Tomb of Nefertari were able to draw on a tradition into which they introduced innovative elements.

The so-called "workmen's village" of Deir el-Medineh lies to the east of the Valley of the Queens. The name belies the fact that the individuals living within its walls were the artisans who were anciently called either "the servants in the place of truth" or "the men of the gang." Responsible for the excavation, decoration, and furnishing of the tombs in both the Valley of the Kings and Valley of the Queens, they were the men who made special vows to Amenhotep I and his mother, Ahmose-Nefertari, the patrons of their endeavors. Although many of these artisans are known by name (because of the plethora of inscribed monuments excavated within their village and elsewhere), one cannot, unfortunately, associate with any degree of confidence any one of these individuals

with the Tomb of Nefertari. The artisans neither signed that work nor left documents that mention their involvement.

Nevertheless, one can suggest, on the basis of the similarities between the stylistic features of her tomb and the representations from the temple of Sety I at Abydos and his tomb in the Valley of the Kings, that the artisans in Nefertari's employ had themselves either worked on her father-in-law's monuments or been trained by those who had. There was, after all, a strong Theban tradition, as we have seen, behind the decoration of her tomb. In fact, the monochromatic style of the paintings in the sarcophagus chamber only finds exact parallels in selected private tombs of the same period.

And if the names of these consummate artisans, who moved beyond the established frontiers of painting by creating original painterly effects, are lost, one can nevertheless sense that their achievement in the Tomb of Nefertari is their tribute to an extraordinary family of Theban women. That tribute is recognizable to all who look at her face and realize the skill with which that face was painted. If all the documents from which her biography can be reconstructed had been lost to the sands of time, and if only one of these renderings of her face had survived, the verdict would still be unanimous. This extraordinary work of art would have to represent the face of a truly extraordinary woman.

# Condition Surveys

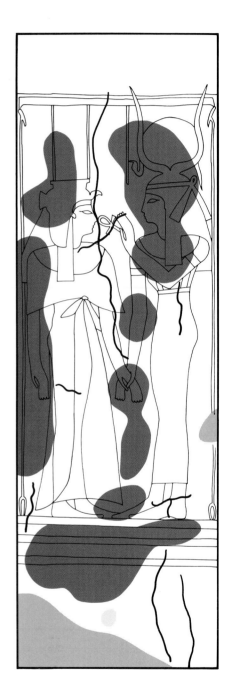

Condition surveys for the east face of Pillar II, Chamber K.

**I.** Condition of Support

delaminated plaster

 cracks

loss of surface plaster

loss of entire strata

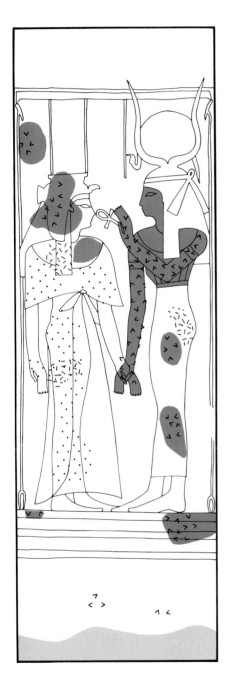

**2.** Condition of Paint Layer

- ⋅ lack of cohesion
- ▮ flaking
- ↘ abrasions
- ∟ loss of paint layer
- ▮ earth sediments and dust

**3.** Previous Interventions

- ⋅ surface treatments
- ▨ mortar splashed on surface
- ▮ filled lacunae

# Checklist
# of the Exhibition

PREPARED BY KAREN MANCHESTER

1. BEAD NET DRESS
From Giza, Tomb G 7440 Z
Fourth dynasty, reign of Khufu
Green(?) and blue faience beads, some on
ancient cord
L: 113 cm; W (reconstructed): 44 cm
Boston, Museum of Fine Arts, Harvard
University-MFA Expedition, inv. 27.1548
Reference: *Mummies and Magic: The Funerary Arts of Ancient Egypt*, exh. cat. (Museum
of Fine Arts, Boston, 1988), pp. 78–79, no. 9.

2. COSMETIC VESSEL
Find spot unknown
Middle Kingdom
Alabaster
H: 7.6 cm; Diam: 7.3 cm
Boston, Museum of Fine Arts, Hay
Collection; Gift of C. Granville Way, inv.
72.505
Unpublished

3. OINTMENT VESSEL
Find spot unknown
New Kingdom
Alabaster
H: 15 cm; Diam: 11 cm
Boston, Museum of Fine Arts, Hay
Collection; Gift of C. Granville Way, inv.
72.507
Unpublished

4. STATUETTE OF ANUBIS ON A LID
Find spot unknown
New Kingdom
Wood
H: 10 cm; W: 8 cm; D: 14 cm
Boston, Museum of Fine Arts inv. W 494
Unpublished

5. STATUETTE OF A *BA*-BIRD
Find spot unknown
New Kingdom
Wood with traces of gesso and paint
H: 12.7 cm
Los Angeles County Museum of Art,
William Randolph Hearst Collection, inv.
51.15.9
Unpublished

6. STATUETTE OF OSIRIS
Find spot unknown
New Kingdom
Wood with gilding
H: 57.2 cm
Los Angeles County Museum of Art, Mr.
and Mrs. Allan C. Balch Fund, inv.
M.60.35.8
Unpublished

7. COSMETIC VESSEL
Find spot unknown
Eighteenth dynasty
Alabaster
H: 15 cm; Diam: 8 cm
Boston, Museum of Fine Arts, Emily
Esther Sears Fund, inv. 03.1539
Unpublished

8. OINTMENT VESSEL
Find spot unknown
Eighteenth dynasty
Alabaster
H: 9 cm; Diam: 7 cm
Boston, Museum of Fine Arts, Gift of the
Estate of Mrs. Francis C. Lowell, inv.
Res.22.236
Unpublished

**9.** BOARD GAME OF TWENTY SQUARES
AND GAMING PIECES
From Thebes
Eighteenth dynasty
Wood, faience
L (board): 28 cm; H (gaming pieces):
1.1–2.5 cm
The Brooklyn Museum, Charles Edwin
Wilbour Fund, inv. 37.93.E, 37.94.E1–
.E23
Reference: E. Pusch, *Das Senet-Brettspiel im
alten Ägypten* (Munich, 1979), pp. 272–73.

**10.** MIRROR WITH HANDLE IN THE SHAPE
OF A CONCUBINE
Find spot unknown
Eighteenth dynasty, reign of
Tuthmosis III
Bronze
H: 38.9 cm; W: 20 cm
Cleveland Museum of Art, Leonard C.
Hanna, Jr. Fund, inv. 83.196
Reference: A. Kozloff, "Mirror, Mirror,"
*Bulletin of the Cleveland Museum of Art*
71(October 1984), pp. 271–75, cover, figs. 3–4.

**11.** UNGUENT JAR AND LID
From Abydos
Eighteenth dynasty, reign of
Tuthmosis III
Alabaster with painted inscription
H: 11.5 cm; Diam: 8 cm
Boston, Museum of Fine Arts, Gift of the
Egypt Exploration Fund, inv. 03.1820 a, b
Reference: W. M. F. Petrie, *Abydos. Part II.
1903* (London, 1903), p. 21, pl. 63, no. 90.

**12.** PAINTER'S PALETTE
Find spot unknown
Eighteenth dynasty, reign of
Amenhotep II
Wood with blue ink inscription, cakes of
red, blue, green, and black pigments
H: 21 cm
Cleveland Museum of Art, Gift of The
John Huntington Art and Polytechnic

Trust, inv. 14.680
Reference: R. Freed, *Ramesses the Great: An
Exhibition in the City of Memphis*, exh. cat.
(Memphis, 1987), p. 103.

**13.** ANKH
From Thebes, Valley of the Kings, Tomb
of Tuthmosis IV (Tomb 43)
Eighteenth dynasty, reign of Tuthmosis IV
Blue faience with dark blue designs
L: 24 cm; W: 13.5 cm
Boston, Museum of Fine Arts, Gift of
Theodore M. Davis, inv. 03.1089
Reference: W. K. Simpson, *The Face of Egypt:
Permanence and Change*, exh. cat. (Katonah
Gallery, 1977), no. 34.

**14.** UNGUENT BOX WITH THE CARTOUCHE
OF NEFERTARI
Find spot unknown, probably Thebes
Nineteenth dynasty, reign of Rameses II
Ivory, ebony
H: 5 cm
New York, The Metropolitan Museum of
Art, Gift of Edward S. Harkness, inv.
26.7.1291
Reference: W. C. Hayes, *The Scepter of Egypt*
(New York, 1959), vol. 2, pp. 343–44.

**15.** LOTUS BUD PENDANT
Find spot unknown
Nineteenth dynasty
Copper, gold
H: 2.2 cm; W: 2.4 cm
Boston, Museum of Fine Arts, Emily
Esther Sears Fund, inv. 04.1956
Unpublished

**16.** STATUE OF AN APE WITH PAWS RAISED
IN ADORATION WITH THE
CARTOUCHE OF RAMESES II
Find spot unknown
Nineteenth dynasty
Stone
H: 18.4 cm

New York, The Metropolitan Museum of
Art, 1966 Fletcher Fund and The Guide
Foundation, Inc. Gift, inv. 66.99.55
Reference: J. D. Cooney, "Egyptian Art in the
Collection of Albert Gallatin," *Journal of Near
Eastern Studies* 12 (1953), p. 17, no. 80.

17. HEADLESS STATUE OF A RAMESIDE
OFFICIAL
From Hierakonpolis
Nineteenth dynasty, reign of Sety I
Gray steatite
H: 23 cm
Boston, Museum of Fine Arts, Gift of
Egypt Exploration Society, inv. 98.1026
References: *Catalogue of the Antiquities from
the Excavations of the EEF at Dendereh and
the ERA at Hierakonpolis*, exh. cat. (University
College London, 1898), pl. 13; Simpson 1977,
no. 28.

18. BUCKLE FROM A BELT(?) WITH THE
CARTOUCHE OF NEFERTARI
Find spot unknown
Nineteenth dynasty, reign of Rameses II
Silver, gold, feldspar, carnelian, blue frit,
glass
H: 4.7 cm; W: 11.5 cm
Boston, Museum of Fine Arts, Emily
Esther Sears Fund, inv. 04.1955
Unpublished

19. ELEMENT FROM A BRACELET WITH
THE CARTOUCHE OF NEFERTARI
Find spot unknown
Nineteenth dynasty, reign of Rameses II
Gold, feldspar, lapis lazuli, carnelian
H: 4 cm; W: 2.5 cm
Boston, Museum of Fine Arts, Emily
Esther Sears Fund, inv. 04.1954
Unpublished

20. *USHABTI* OF RAMESES II
From Thebes, Deir el-Bahari, Tomb 320
Nineteenth dynasty, reign of Rameses II

Wood
H: 31.8 cm; W: 8.7 cm
The Brooklyn Museum, Charles Edwin
Wilbour Fund, inv. 08.480.5
References: *The De Potter Collection* (n.p.,
n.d.), no. A54; J.-F. and L. Aubert, *Statuettes
égyptiennes: Chaouabties. Ouchebties*
(Paris, 1974), pp. 81–82.

21. OSTRAKON SHOWING RAMESES II
NURSED BY A GODDESS
Find spot unknown, perhaps Deir
el-Medineh
Nineteenth dynasty, reign of Rameses II
Painted limestone flake
H: 31.4 cm
The Cleveland Museum of Art, Gift in
Honor of James N. Sherwin, Trustee,
1957–1971, inv. 87.156
Reference: "Year in Review for 1987," *Bulletin
of the Cleveland Museum of Art* 75, no. 2
(February 1988), pp. 46, 65, no. 5.

22. RELIEF REPRESENTATION OF
RAMESES II
From Abydos, Temple of Rameses II
Nineteenth dynasty, reign of Rameses II
Painted limestone
H: 42.5 cm; W: 36.5 cm; D: 9 cm
The Brooklyn Museum inv. 11.670
References: J. D. Cooney, "Gods Bearing Gifts
for the King," *Bulletin of the Cleveland
Museum of Art* 54, no. 9 (November 1967), pp.
289f., fig. 5; R. Fazinni, *Images for Eternity*
(Brooklyn, 1975), p. 91, no. 77; H. T. Frank,
*Discovering the Biblical World* (Maplewood,
N.J., 1975), p. 56; *Ancient Egyptian Art in the
Brooklyn Museum* (Brooklyn, 1989), no. 61.

23. STATUE OF NEFERTARI
Find spot unknown
Nineteenth dynasty, reign of Rameses II
Granite
H: 94 cm
San Bernardino, Harer Family Trust
Collection

References: J. Pijóan, *Summa artis*, vol. 3: *El arte egipcio* (Madrid, 1932), p. 278, fig. 363; C. Aldred, *Egyptian Art* (New York, 1980), p. 186; J. Herbert (ed.), *Christie's Review of the Season 1979* (London, 1980), p. 421; H. Satzinger, "Der heilige Stab also Kraftquelle des Königs," *Jahrbuch der Kunsthistorischen Sammlungen in Wien* 77 (1981), p. 33 (Dok. B4); C. Chadefaud, *Les Statues porte-enseignes de l'Egypte ancienne* (Paris, 1982), p. 98 (PEC. 4); C. Desroches-Noblecourt, "Touy, mère de Ramsès II, la reine Tanedjmy et les reliques de l'expérience amarnienne," in *Colloques internationaux du C.N.R.S. no. 595— L'Egyptologie en 1979: Axes prioritaires de recherches II* (Paris, 1982), pp. 238–39, fig. 65; G. D. Scott, *Temple, Tomb and Dwelling: Egyptian Antiquities from the Harer Family Trust Collection*, exh. cat. (University Art Gallery, California State University, San Bernardino, 1992), pp. 132–34.

24. FRAGMENT FROM A STATUETTE OF
    RAMESES II
    Find spot unknown
    Nineteenth dynasty, reign of Rameses II
    Red jasper
    H: 4.5 cm
    New York, The Metropolitan Museum of
    Art, Gift of Mr. and Mrs. Charles D.
    Kelekian, inv. 1980.517
    Unpublished

25. BLOCK STATUE INSCRIBED FOR PRINCE
    MENTUHERKOPESHEF
    From Bubastis
    Nineteenth dynasty, reign of Rameses II
    Black granite
    H: 88 cm
    Boston, Museum of Fine Arts, Gift of
    Egypt Exploration Fund, inv. 88.748
    References: E. Naville, "Les fouilles du Delta
    pendant l'hiver de 1887," *Recueil de travaux
    relatifs à la philologie et assyriennes pour
    servir du Bulletin à la Mission Française du
    Caire* 10 (1888), p. 59.

26. SARCOPHAGUS
    From Thebes
    Twenty-first dynasty
    Wood, gesso, pigments
    L: 183 cm
    Los Angeles County Museum of Art,
    Purchase with funds provided by Mr. and
    Mrs. John Jewett Garland, inv.
    M.47.3 A–B
    Unpublished

27. URAEUS
    Find spot unknown
    Late Period
    Bronze
    H: 13 cm
    Boston, Museum of Fine Arts, Hay
    Collection; Gift of C. Granville Way, inv.
    72.4442
    Unpublished

28. STATUETTE OF SEKHMET OR HATHOR
    AS LIONESS AND EYE OF RE
    Find spot unknown
    Twenty-sixth dynasty
    Bronze
    H: 25.4 cm
    Los Angeles County Museum of Art,
    William Randolph Hearst Collection, inv.
    50.4.14
    Unpublished

29. STATUETTE OF WADJET
    Find spot unknown
    Twenty-sixth dynasty
    Bronze
    H: 33 cm
    Los Angeles County Museum of Art,
    William Randolph Hearst Collection, inv.
    50.37.14
    Unpublished

**30.** PECTORAL IN THE FORM OF THE
WINGED GODDESS ISIS
From Nuri (modern Sudan), Tomb of
King Amarinatakilebte
Late sixth century B.C.
Gold
H: 6.9 cm; W: 16.7 cm
Boston, Museum of Fine Arts, Harvard
University-MFA Expedition, inv. 20.276
Reference: D. Dunham, *The Royal Cemeteries
of Kush II. Nuri* (Boston, 1955), p. 155.

**31.** SISTRUM
Find spot unknown
Thirtieth dynasty
Bronze
H: 21.3 cm
Cleveland Museum of Art, Gift of The
John Huntington Art and Polytechnic
Trust, inv. 20.1990
Unpublished

**32.** FRAGMENT FROM THE WRAPPINGS OF
A MUMMY WITH THE FIGURE OF
NEKHBET
Find spot unknown
Ptolemaic or Roman Period
Painted *cartonnage*
H: 24 cm; W: 46 cm
Boston, Museum of Fine Arts, Hay
Collection; Gift of C. Granville Way
Unpublished

**33.** STATUETTE OF THOTH
Find spot unknown
Ptolemaic Period
Faience
H: 5 cm
Los Angeles County Museum of Art,
Anonymous gift, inv. M.80.200.3
Unpublished

**34.** STATUETTE OF ISIS NURSING THE
INFANT HORUS
Find spot unknown
Twenty-sixth dynasty–Ptolemaic Period

Bronze
H: 16.9 cm
San Bernardino, Harer Family Trust
Collection
Reference: *Temple, Tomb and Dwelling:
Egyptian Antiquities from the Harer Family
Trust Collection*, exh. cat. (University Art
Gallery, California State University, San
Bernardino, 1992), pp. 58–59, no. 31 A.

**35.** STATUETTE OF OSIRIS
Find spot unknown
Late Period
Bronze
H: 20 cm
San Bernardino, Harer Family Trust
Collection
Reference: *Temple, Tomb and Dwelling:
Egyptian Antiquities from the Harer Family
Trust Collection*, exh. cat. (University Art
Gallery, California State University, San
Bernardino, 1992), pp. 141, 143, no. 89.

**36.** STATUETTE OF PTAH
Find spot unknown
Late Period–Ptolemaic Period
Bronze
H: 11.4 cm
San Bernardino, Harer Family Trust
Collection
Reference: *Temple, Tomb and Dwelling:
Egyptian Antiquities from the Harer Family
Trust Collection*, exh. cat. (University Art
Gallery, California State University, San
Bernardino, 1992), pp. 58, 60, no. 32 A.

**37.** STATUETTE OF NEITH
Find spot unknown
Late Period–Ptolemaic Period
Bronze
H: 24.2 cm
San Bernardino, Harer Family Trust
Collection
Reference: *Temple, Tomb and Dwelling:
Egyptian Antiquities from the Harer Family
Trust Collection*, exh. cat. (University Art

Gallery, California State University, San
Bernardino, 1992), pp. 58, 60, no. 32 B.

**38.** STATUETTE OF BAST (OR BASTET)
Find spot unknown
Late Period–Ptolemaic Period
Bronze
H: 15.8 cm
San Bernardino, Harer Family Trust
Collection
Reference: *Temple, Tomb and Dwelling:*
*Egyptian Antiquities from the Harer Family*
*Trust Collection*, exh. cat. (University Art
Gallery, California State University, San
Bernardino, 1992), pp. 58, 60, no. 32 C; C.
Ede, *Collecting Antiquities* (London, 1983), p.
94, no. 246.

**39.** SET OF FOUR CANOPIC JARS
Find spot unknown
Third Intermediate Period
Limestone with black ink inscriptions
H (average): 23 cm
San Bernardino, Harer Family Trust
Collection
Reference: *Temple, Tomb and Dwelling:*
*Egyptian Antiquities from the Harer Family*
*Trust Collection*, exh. cat. (University Art
Gallery, California State University, San
Bernardino, 1992), p. 90, no. 50.

# Glossary

### ABU SIMBEL

A site located south of the Tropic of Cancer where two temples, the northern one dedicated to Nefertari, the southern one dedicated to Rameses II, were cut entirely from the living rock. These monuments were dismantled and reconstructed in the 1960s on ground above their original location by an international team under the auspices of UNESCO. This was done to protect them from the rising waters of Lake Nasser, which was formed as a result of the building of the High Dam at Aswan.

### AMARNA PERIOD

The name El Amarna, derived from that of a local tribe, is generally applied to the ancient site of Akhetaton, "the horizon of the *aton*," Pharaoh Akhenaten's capital. The name is used by extension as a label for that brief epoch during the eighteenth dynasty when his religious reforms were in force.

### AMUN

Of uncertain origin, this god, often represented as a man, rose to prominence during the eighteenth dynasty to become the supreme deity of Thebes, then the nation's capital city.

### ANATOLIA

The name applied to the Hittite heartland, which corresponds roughly to central and eastern modern Turkey.

### *ATON*

The ancient Egyptian designation for the sun disk, which, personified, was worshiped as the great deity of creation by the pharaoh Akhenaten.

### ATUM

Originally a sun god worshiped at Heliopolis, this deity became one of the guarantors of kingship during the New Kingdom.

### BITUMEN

A tarlike mineral substance occurring as natural asphalt and put to various uses by the ancient Egyptians.

### DELTA

The fourth letter of the Greek alphabet, shaped like a triangle and used to describe the configuration of the Nile's flood plane, the base of which roughly corresponds to the Mediterranean coast and the apex of which is located in the vicinity of Cairo.

### *DJED* AMULET

A hieroglyph representing a bundle of stalks tied together that was reproduced in various media as a symbol connoting stability, endurance, and the like.

### GOD'S WIFE OF AMUN

A religious title conferred on wives or daughters of the pharaohs of the New Kingdom. It made manifest the mythic ideal of the female regenerative forces that had to combine with those of the male principle in order to insure the maintenance and perpetuation of the cosmic powers responsible for creation, renewal, and resurrection.

### HATHOR

A goddess of many functions and attributes who was often depicted either as a cow-headed woman or as a woman with cow's ears and horns. Known as the "Golden One," she was said to suckle pharaohs and was later identified by the Greeks as Aphrodite.

## HATTI

The name given to the indigenous peoples of the Anatolian highlands who were conquered by the Hittites.

## HIEROGLYPH

Composed of two ancient Greek words meaning "sacred writing," this term is used to designate the pictographic writings of the ancient Egyptians.

## HITTITES

The name given to the Indo-European invaders of the Anatolian highlands who established an empire during the course of the second millennium B.C. and challenged the supremacy of Egypt in the Middle East during the eighteenth and nineteenth dynasties.

## HORUS

A falcon deity, originally worshiped as a sky god, who was later both identified with the reigning pharaoh and regarded as the son of the deities Isis and Osiris.

## HYKSOS

The English rendering of the ancient Egyptian phrase meaning "rulers of the hill countries." This phrase was applied to a Semitic people who took advantage of Egypt's instability at the close of the Middle Kingdom by invading the country and establishing a strong military presence in the eastern delta.

## ISIS

The divine wife of Osiris and mother of Horus who gradually became the chief protector-goddess, assimilating to herself many of the attributes of Hathor and eventually becoming the supreme Egyptian deity during the Roman imperial period.

## KARNAK

A name of uncertain origin applied to the extraordinary complex of temples located on the east bank of the Nile River at Thebes and forming the northern adjunct of the Luxor temples just to the south. Here are found three principal precincts, dedicated to Montu, the war god; Amun, the state god; and Mut, Amun's chief consort, respectively.

## LATE PERIOD

This is the designation for the last epoch of Egypt's history, the exact chronological limits of which are debated. A broad interpretation places its beginning with the advent of the twenty-fifth dynasty and its end with the collapse of Roman rule. More narrowly defined, this period encompasses only the twenty-sixth to the thirty-first dynasties, corresponding roughly to those periods between 664 and 332 B.C. during which Egypt was ruled, in the main, by native pharaohs.

## LOWER EGYPT

By convention, the area of Egypt roughly corresponding to the delta is so termed because the ancient Egyptians themselves referred to their country as "The Two Lands." The designation is confusing until one realizes that both it and the corresponding southern region, termed Upper Egypt, are described in terms of the Nile's current, which flows from south to north.

## LUXOR

A place-name thought to derive either from the Arabic word for "the palaces" or the Latin for "camp." This temple complex on the east bank of the Nile River at Thebes forms the southern adjunct of the northern complex at Karnak. It was here that the cult of Amun, as a fertility god associated with Min, was celebrated together with that of the reigning pharaoh's life forces.

MIDDLE KINGDOM

The ancient Egyptians themselves divided their history into epochs separated by periods of discord. The second major period of unification, standing chronologically between the first, or Old Kingdom, and the third, or New Kingdom, is so designated by convention. It was a period during which the cult of Osiris spread, and nomarchs, or provincial governors, challenged the authority of the crown.

MIN

The primeval god of Coptos, a site just north of Karnak, was later revered as a god of fertility and, in the New Kingdom, was closely associated with Amun. He is represented as an ithyphallic male figure holding a flail. Lettuce was associated with him as an aphrodisiac.

MISSIONE ARCHEOLOGICA ITALIANA IN EGITTO

"The Italian Archaeological Expedition in Egypt" was the official title of the umbrella organization that sponsored, among other endeavors, the excavations of Ernesto Schiaparelli in the Valley of the Queens.

MUMMY

A word of uncertain origin, perhaps derived from a Persian word for "bitumen." It was then applied to the preserved mortal remains of the ancient Egyptians, because the appearance of the ancient balms and unguents reminded early commentators of that naturally occurring pitch.

MUT

The divine wife of the state god Amun whose principal cult center was the southernmost of the three precincts at Karnak. She was represented either as a vulture or as a woman.

NEKHBET

This goddess, who sometimes appears as a vulture, had her cult center at Elkab, to the south of Luxor, where she was, from very early times, worshiped as the tutelary deity of Upper Egypt.

NEPHTHYS

The sister of the goddess Isis, often depicted as a woman, who came to represent mourning in general because of her lamentations at the death of the god Osiris.

NEW KINGDOM

The designation for the third, and most recent, of the periods of Egypt's unification and stability, a time of empire, of a great flowering in the arts and architecture, of religious experiment, and the like.

NUBIA

Derived from the ancient Egyptian word for "gold," this term is applied to the geographic region extending roughly from the First Cataract of the Nile in Egypt well into modern Sudan. Its inhabitants, termed Nubians, developed their own culture in tandem with that of the Egyptians, although at times Nubia was either under Egypt's control or that country's ruler.

OLD KINGDOM

This is the name given to the first, and chronologically oldest, of the three periods of Egypt's unification and stability. It was a time during which the pharaohs were absolute monarchs for whom the grandest of the pyramids were constructed as tombs.

OSIRIS

The husband of Isis, who gathered the parts of his body after he was dismembered by Seth, his evil brother. Because of her ministrations, Osiris was reassembled and posthumously conceived his son and successor, Horus. For these reasons, he was considered to be the god of the underworld and offered the hope of resurrection to the faithful.

PTAH

The creator god of Memphis, located to the southwest of modern Cairo, who was represented as a mummiform man and later equated by the Greeks with their god Hephaestus.

RE

Like Atum, a manifestation of the sun god of Heliopolis who was often linked to other deities, such as Amun, in cults aspiring to universality.

REHORAKHTY

A god in the form of a falcon whose name, "Horus of the Two Horizons," represents the union of Re and Horus as a universal solar deity.

SARCOPHAGUS

From the ancient Greek words meaning "flesh-eater," this term is used to denote any coffinlike container into which the mortal remains of the deceased are placed for interment.

SENET

From the ancient Egyptian verb meaning "to pass [someone or something]," the word is applied to a board game consisting of thirty squares with movable gaming pieces anciently termed "the dancers." In certain funerary contexts, the deceased is represented playing this game alone. His/her unseen opponent symbolizes Fate,

who must be defeated in order to gain immortality in the hereafter.

SILSILA WEST

A site on both sides of the Nile River just north of Aswan. On the west bank are found several shrines, including the *speos*, or rock-cut chapel, commissioned by the pharaoh Horemhab, while the east bank contains the quarries that were exploited from the time of the New Kingdom until the end of the Roman imperial period.

SISTRUM

Via the principle of onomatopoeia, this ancient Egyptian word for "sacred rattle" imitates the swishing sound such musical instruments made when played by priestesses in rituals designed to calm the savage fury of the goddesses representing the avenging powers of deities such as Re.

STELA

An ancient Greek word meaning "an upright stone." It is applied by convention to monuments, usually freestanding, in a variety of media and sizes, to which inscriptions were added, generally in commemoration of an event or in honor of a deceased person.

*TA SET NEFERU*

The ancient Egyptian phrase designating the area in Western Thebes today called the Valley of the Queens. Although translated as either "The Place of Beauty" or "The Place of Perfection," the phrase should be rendered into English as "The Place Where the Royal Children Repose," according to recent scholars.

THEBES

The name given to the southern region of the Nile River's great bend by the ancient Greeks, because the accumulated effect of the entrances of the area's temple complexes, particularly those at Karnak, reminded them of their own mythological "hundred-gated Thebes."

THOTH

The Egyptian god of wisdom and writing, often depicted as an ibis-headed male figure to whom scribes traditionally addressed a prayer before beginning their work.

UPPER EGYPT

This name is applied to the Nile's valley, beginning just south of modern Cairo and extending to the vicinity of Aswan. Because the river flows from south to north, this part of the country, from the vantage of the delta, is located upstream.

URAEUS

Via the ancient Greek word for "tail," this term is generally applied to the cobra, which the ancient Egyptians associated with Wadjet, the tutelary goddess of Lower Egypt, and which, together with Nekhbet, often decorated the brow of the pharaoh. By extension, the cobra might be employed as a motif connoting protection in a general sense.

USHABTI

The English transliteration for the most recent of the three ancient Egyptian words generally translated as "funerary figurines," which first appear in the Egyptian cultural record near the beginning of the Middle Kingdom. The figurines' function was to serve as surrogates for the deceased, called upon to perform specific but onerous tasks in the hereafter as specified in Spell 6 of the collection of funerary texts termed *The Book of the Dead*.

WADJET

The tutelary goddess of Lower Egypt whose cult center was located in the delta city of Buto. She was represented as a uraeus, or cobra.

# Selected Bibliography

**I.** The Conservation of the Wall Paintings

Burns, G., and K. M. Wilson-Yang. *The Tomb of Nefertari, Valley of the Queens and Its Conservation Problems.* Toronto, 1981. Preliminary report, Archaeometric Laboratory.

Burton, H. *In the Valley of the Tombs of the Queens.* New York, Metropolitan Museum of Art, Egyptian Expedition. Collection of photographs taken between 1920 and 1923.

Campbell, C. *Two Theban Queens: Nefertari and Ty-ti, and Their Tombs.* London, 1909.

Corzo, M. A., coord. ed. *Wall Paintings of the Tomb of Nefertari: Scientific Studies for Their Conservation.* Cairo and Century City, 1987. First progress report.

Helck, W., and E. Otto. "Nofretere." In *Lexikon der Ägyptologie.* Vol. 4. Wiesbaden, 1982. Pp. 518–19.

Leblanc, C. *Ta Set Neferou: Une Nécropole de Thèbes-ouest et son histoire.* Vol. 1. Cairo, 1989.

Mekhitarian, A. *La Peinture égyptienne.* Geneva, 1954. Photographs by M. C. Emmer.

Michalowski, A., ed., and S. Rakowski, trans. *The Tomb of Queen Nefertari: Problems of Conserving Wall Paintings: Diagnosing the State of Preservation and Conservator's Proposals.* Warsaw, 1973. Published by Working Group of the State Ateliers for the Preservation of Historical Property.

Mond, R. "A Method of Photographing Mural Decorations." *Photographic Journal,* n.s. 57 (January 1933).

Plenderleith, H. J. *United Arab Republic Conservation Problems: April 1970.* Paris, 1970. UNESCO report, sect. 2, serial no. 1914/BMS.RD/CLT.

Schiaparelli, E. *Relazione sui lavori della Missione Archeologica Italiana in Egitto (Anni 1903–20).* Vol. 1, *Esplorazione della "Valle delle Regine" nella necropoli di Tebe.* Turin, 1923.

Stopperlaëre, A. "Dégradations et restaurations des peintures murales égyptiennes." In *Annales du Service des Antiquités de l'Egypte* 40 (1940), pp. 941–50.

Thausing, G., and H. Goedicke. *Nofretari: A Documentation of Her Tomb and Its Decoration.* Graz, 1971. Photographs by E. Ritter.

Torraca, G. *ICCROM Mission to the Tomb of Queen Nefetarri, February, 1978: Conclusions of the Report.* Rome, 1978. International Centre for the Study of the Preservation and Restoration of Cultural Property report no. 35, GT/EA.

Wilson-Yang, K. M., T. C. Billard, and G. Burns. "Chemistry and Physics in the Tomb of Nefertari." *Journal of the Society for the Study of Egyptian Antiquities* 12 (1982), pp. 9–11. University of Toronto report, 1977–81.

**2.** Some Royal Women of the Seventeenth and Eighteenth Dynasties

Aldred, C. "Egypt: The Amarna Period and the End of the Eighteenth Dynasty." In I. E. S. Edwards et al., eds. *The Cambridge Ancient History.* 3rd ed. Vol. 2, pt. 2, *History of the Middle East and the Aegean Region c. 1380–1000 B.C.* Cambridge, 1975.

———. "Ahmose-Nofertari Again." In H. De Meulenaere and L. Limme, eds. *Musées Royaux d'Art et d'Histoire: Artibus Aegypti: Studia in honorem Bernardi V. Bothmer a collegis amicis discipulis conscripta.* Brussels, 1983. Pp. 7–14.

———. *Akhenaten: King of Egypt.* London, 1988.

Barta, W. "Akencheres und die Witwe des Nibhururia." *Göttinger Miszellen* 62 (1983), pp. 15–21.

Bongrani Fanfoni, L. "Ay, Tutankhamen e Mutnedjemet." *Studi classici e orientali* 30 (1980), pp. 61–67.

Černy, J. "Le Culte d'Amenophis Ier chèz les ouvriers de la nécropole thébaine." *Bulletin de l'Institut Français d'Archéologie Orientale* 27 (1927), pp. 159–203.

Gitton, M. "Nouvelles remarques sur la stèle de donation d'Ahmès Néfertary." *Bulletin de l'Institut Français d'Archéologie Orientale* 79 (1979), pp. 327–31.

———. *Les Divines épouses de la 18e dynastie.* Centre de Recherches d'Histoire Ancienne, 61. Paris, 1984.

Helck, W. *Kleine ägyptische Texte: Historisch-biographische Texte der 2. Zwischenzeit und neue Texte der 18. Dynastie.* Wiesbaden, 1975.

Manniche, L. "The Complexion of Queen Ahmosi Nefertere." *Acta orientalia* 40 (1979), pp. 11–19.

Martin, G. T. *A Bibliography of the Amarna Period and Its Aftermath: The Reigns of Akhenaten, Smenkhkare, Tutankhamun and Ay (c. 1350–1321 B.C.).* London, 1991.

Redford, D. B. *Akhenaten: The Heretic King.* Princeton, 1984.

Robins, G. "A Critical Examination of the Theory That the Right to the Throne of Ancient Egypt Passed through the Female Line in the 18th Dynasty." *Göttinger Miszellen* 62 (1983), pp. 67–77.

———. "The Role of the Royal Family in the 18th Dynasty up to the End of the Reign of Amenhotep III: 1. Queens." *Wepwawet: Papers in Egyptology* (Summer 1986), pp. 10–14.

Schulman, A. R. "The Nubian Wars of Akhenaton." In *Colloques internationaux du C.N.R.S. no. 595—L'Egyptologie en 1979: Axes prioritaires de recherches II.* Paris, 1982. Pp. 299–316.

Thomas, A. P. *Akhenaten's Egypt.* Aylesbury, Bucks., 1988.

Troy, L. *Patterns of Queenship in Ancient Egyptian Myth and History.* Acta universitatis upsaliensis boreas: Uppsala Studies in Ancient Mediterranean and Near Eastern Civilization, 14. Uppsala, 1986.

Vandersleyen, C. *Les Guerres d'Amosis: Fondateur de la XVIIIe dynastie.* Monographies Reine Elisabeth, 1. Brussels, 1975.

**3.** Nefertari as Chief Queen and Principal Wife

Breasted, J. H. *Ancient Records of Egypt: Historical Documents from the Earliest Times to the Persian Conquest, Collected, Edited, and Translated with Commentary III: The Nineteenth Dynasty.* Chicago, 1906.

Černy, J. In C. Aldred, "The End of the Amarna Period." *Journal of Egyptian Archaeology* 43 (1957), p. 33, n. 1.

Cruz-Uribe, E. "The Father of Ramses I: OI 11456." *Journal of Near Eastern Studies* 37 (1978), pp. 237–44.

Desroches-Noblecourt, C. "Touy, mère de Ramsès II, la reine Tanedjmy et les reliques de l'expérience amarnienne." In *Colloques internationaux du C.N.R.S. no. 595— L'Egyptologie en 1979: Axes prioritaires de recherches II.* Paris, 1982. Pp. 227–43.

———, and C. Kuentz. *Le Petit temple d'Abou Simbel I: Etude, archéologique et épigraphique, essai d'interprétation.* Ministère de la Culture, Centre de Documentation et d'Etudes sur l'Ancienne Egypte, Mémoires, 1. Cairo, 1968.

El-Alfi, M. "Ramesside Divinities of Nubia." *Discussions in Egyptology* 18 (1990), pp. 21–26.

Freed, R. *Ramesses the Great: An Exhibition in the City of Memphis.* Exh. cat. Memphis, 1987.

Hari, R. *Horemheb et Reine Moutnedjemet ou la fin d'une dynastie.* Geneva, 1965.

———. "Mout-Nefertari, épouse de Ramses II: Une descendante de l'hérétique Ai?" *Aegyptus* 59 (1979), pp. 3–7.

Janssen, J. J. "La Reine Nefertari et la succession de Ramsès II par Merenptah." *Chronique d'Egypte* 38 (1963), pp. 30–36.

Kitchen, K. A. *Pharaoh Triumphant: The Life and Times of Ramesses II.* Warminster, Wilts., 1982.

Legrain, G. *Service des Antiquités de l'Egypte: Catalogue général des antiquités égyptiennes du Musée du Caire: Nos. 42139–42191: Statues et statuettes de rois et de particuliers.* Vol. 2. Cairo, 1909.

Murnane, W. J. *The Road to Kadesh: A Historical Interpretation of the Battle Reliefs of King Sety I at Karnak.* 2nd rev. ed. The Oriental Institute of the University of Chicago: Studies in Ancient Oriental Civilization, 42. Chicago, 1990.

**4.** On the Nature of Egyptian Painting

Andrews, C. *Ancient Egyptian Jewellery.* London, 1990.

Assmann, J. "Zweites Beispiel: Genese und Verfall eines neuen Stils in der Flachbildkunst des neuen Reiches." In idem and G. Burkard, eds. *5000 Jahre Ägypten: Genese und Permanenz pharaonischer Kunst.* Nussloch, 1983. Pp. 21–32.

Baines, J. "Color Terminology and Color Classification: Ancient Egyptian Color Terminology and Polychromy." *American Anthropologist* 87 (1985), pp. 282–97.

———. "Theories and Universals of Representation: Heinrich Schäfer and Egyptian Art." *Art History* 8 (1985), pp. 1–25.

———. "Restricted Knowledge, Hierarchy, and Decorum: Modern Perceptions and Ancient Institutions." *Journal of the American Research Center in Egypt* 27 (1990), pp. 1–23.

———. "Egyptian Myth and Discourse: Myth, Gods, and the Early Written and Iconographic Record." *Journal of Near Eastern Studies* 50 (1991), pp. 81–105.

Bierbrier, M. *The Tomb-Builders of the Pha-raohs*. New York, 1982.

Cherpion, N. "Quelques jalons pour une histoire de la peinture thébaine." *Bulletin de la Société Française d'Egyptologie* 110 (1987), pp. 27–47.

DeGaris Davies, N. *Two Ramesside Tombs at Thebes*. Robb de Peyster Tytus Memorial Series, 5. New York, 1927.

Della Monica, M. *La Classe ouvrière sous les pharaons: Etude du village de Deir al Medineh*. Paris, 1980.

Fischer, H. G. "Varia Aegyptiaca I: Yellow-Skinned Representations of Men in the Old Kingdom." *Journal of the American Research Center in Egypt* 2 (1963), pp. 17–22.

Goodman, N. "Art and Authenticity." In D. Dutton, ed. *The Forger's Art: Forgery and the Philosophy of Art*. Berkeley, 1983. Pp. 93–114.

Hornung, E. "Hieroglyphen: Die Welt im Spiegel der Zeichen." *ERANOS 1986 Jahrbuch-Yearbook-Annales* 55 [1988], pp. 403–38.

James, T. G. H. *Egyptian Paintings and Draw-ings in the British Museum*. Cambridge, Mass., 1986.

Keller, K. "The Draughtsmen of Deir el-Midena: A Preliminary Report." *Newsletter of the American Research Center in Egypt* 115 (Summer 1981), pp. 7–14.

Manniche, L. "The Body Colours of Gods and Men in Inlaid Jewellery and Related Objects from the Tomb of Tutankhamun." *Acta orientalia* 43 (1982), pp. 5–13.

Peck, W. H. *Egyptian Drawings*. New York, 1978.

Porter, B., and R. L. B. Moss. *Topographical Bibliography of Ancient Egyptian Hieroglyphic Texts, Reliefs, and Paintings*. Vol. 1, *The Theban Necropolis, Part 2: Royal Tombs and Smaller Cemeteries*. 2nd ed. Oxford, 1964.

Robins, G. *Egyptian Paintings and Relief*. Aylesbury, Bucks., 1986.

Staehelin, E. "Zu den Farben der Hieroglyphen." *Göttinger Miszellen* 14 (1974), pp. 49–53.

Valbelle, D. *"Les Ouvriers de la tombe:" Deir el-Médineh à l'époque ramesside*. Institut Français d'Archéologie Orientale: Bibliothèque d'étude, 96. Cairo, 1985.

Wilkinson, C. K. *Egyptian Wall Paintings: The Metropolitan Museum's Collection of Facsimi-les*. New York, 1983. Catalogue compiled by M. Hill.

**5.** AN ASSESSMENT OF THE WALL PAINTINGS

Curto, S. *L'antico Egitto nel Museo Egizio di Torino*. Turin, 1984.

Desroches-Noblecourt, C., et al. *Ramses le Grand*. Exh. cat. Galeries Nationales du Grand Palais, Paris, 1976.

Farina, G. *Ministero della Educazione Nazio-nale, Direzione Generale della Antichità e Belle Arti. Itinerari dei musei e monumenti d'Italia: Il regio Museo di Antichità di Torino, sezione egizia*. Rome, 1938.

Leblanc, C. "Les tombes no. 58 [Anonyme] et no. 60 [Nebet-Taouy] dans la Vallée des Reines [Rapport préliminaire]." *Annales du Service des Antiquités de l'Egypte* 69 (1983), pp. 39–52.

————. "*T3 st nfrw*—Une nécropole et son histoire." In S. Schoske, ed. *Akten des Vierten Internationalen Ägyptologen Kongresses München 1985* 2 [ = *Studien zur altägyptischen Kultur Beihefte* 2 (1988)], pp. 89–99.

————. 1989 (see under section 1 above).

Reeves, C. N. *Valley of the Kings: The Decline of a Royal Necropolis*. London, 1990.

Schiaparelli, E. 1923 (see under section 1 above).

Thausing, G., and H. Goedicke, 1971 (see under section 1 above).

# The Joint Egyptian Antiquities Organization-Getty Conservation Institute Nefertari Conservation Project

## Project Members 1985–1992

### EXECUTIVE BODY

Dr. Mohamed Ibrahim Bakr
Chairman
Egyptian Antiquities Organization

Mr. Miguel Angel Corzo
Director
The Getty Conservation Institute

The late Dr. Ahmed Kadry
Former Chairman
Egyptian Antiquities Organization

Mr. Luis Monreal
Former Director
The Getty Conservation Institute

Dr. Gamal Moukhtar
Former Chairman
Egyptian Antiquities Organization

The late Dr. Sayed Tawfik
Former Chairman
Egyptian Antiquities Organization

### SCIENTIFIC TEAM

Eng. Farrag Abd el-Mouttaleb
Eng. Nabil Abd el-Samia
Dr. Neville Agnew
Prof. Mokhtar S. Ammar
Prof. Hideo Arai
Dr. Omar el-Arini
Mr. Motawe Balbouch
Dr. Kamal Barakat
Dr. Farouk el-Baz
Ms. Asmaa A. el-Deeb
Dr. Feisal A. H. Esmael
Dr. Gaballa A. Gaballa
Dr. Essam H. Ghanem
Dr. Hanl A. Hamroush
Dr. B. Issawi
Dr. Po-Ming Lin
Mr. Shin Maekawa
Prof. Modesto Montoto
Dr. Shawki Nakhla
Dr. Frank Preusser
Dr. Saleh A. Saleh
Mr. Michael Schilling
Dr. Wafa Seddia
Dr. Mohamed el-Sougayar

### CONSERVATION TEAM

Profs. Paolo Mora and Laura Mora, Directors
Abd el-Rady Abd el-Moniem
Abd el-Nasser Ahmed
Lorenza D'Alessandro
Giorgio Capriotti
Luigi de Cesaris
Giuseppe Giordano
Ahmed-Ali Hussein
Lutfi Khaled
Adriano Luzi
Gamal Mahgoub
Hussein Mohamed-Ali
Talat Mohrem
Stephen Rickerby
Sayed A. el-Shahat
Christina Vazio

### PHOTOGRAPHER

Guillermo Aldana

### RESEARCH

Dr. Mahasti Afshar

### MANAGEMENT

Mr. Ahmed Abd el-Radi
Ms. Mary Helmy
Mr. Romany Helmy
Dr. Mohamed Nasr
Mr. Eduardo Porta
Ms. Laura Sanders
Ms. Inée Yang Slaughter

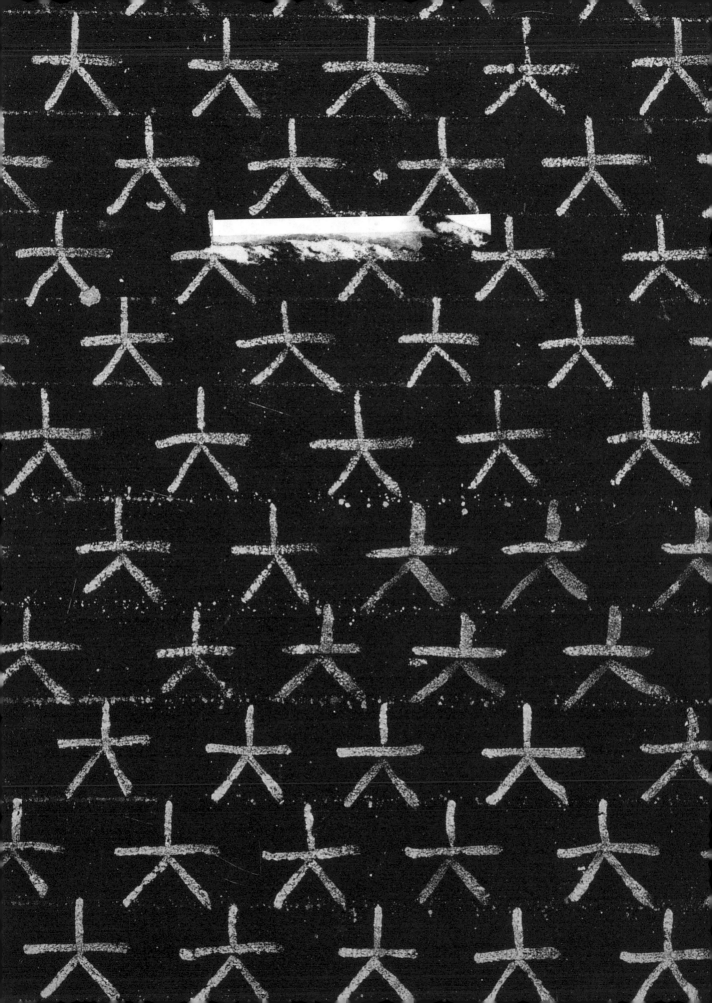